SECURITY

LUCIA ZEDNER

Routledge
Taylor & Francis Group

LONDON AND NEW YORK

First published 2009
by Routledge
2 Park Square, Milton Park, Abingdon, Oxon OX14 4RN

Simultaneously published in the USA and Canada
by Routledge
270 Madison Ave, New York, NY 10016

Routledge is an imprint of the Taylor & Francis Group, an informa business

© 2009 Lucia Zedner

Typeset in Garamond 3 by RefineCatch Limited, Bungay, Suffolk
Printed and bound in Great Britain by
TJ International Ltd, Padstow, Cornwall

British Library Cataloguing in Publication Data
A catalogue record for this book is available from the British Library

Library of Congress Cataloging in Publication Data
Zedner, Lucia.
Security / Lucia Zedner.
p. cm.
Includes bibliographical reference and index.
1. Security systems industry.   2. Security systems.   3. National
security.   4. Security, International.   I. Title.
HD9999.S452Z43 2009
363.1—dc22
2008036736

ISBN10: 0–415–39175–X (hbk)
ISBN10: 0–415–39176–8 (pbk)
ISBN10: 0–203–87113–8 (ebk)

ISBN13: 978–0–415–39175–7 (hbk)
ISBN13: 978–0–415–39176–4 (pbk)
ISBN13: 978–0–203–87113–3 (ebk)

For Naomi and Esther

CONTENTS

ACKNOWLEDGEMENTS

I thank Tim Newburn for inviting me to contribute to the *Routledge Key Ideas in Criminology* series. I gratefully acknowledge the generous support of the British Academy, whose award of a Research Readership made this book possible. Thanks are due to members of the Security reading group at Oxford – Andrew Ashworth, Benjamin Goold, Liora Lazarus, and Ian Loader – for the stimulating debates we have had over many years. Ben and Ian deserve special thanks for reading and commenting on this book in its entirety, as do Laurence Lustgarten, Conor O'Reilly, and my husband Joshua Getzler. The book is better for their criticisms and I am hugely grateful to them. Jörg Friedrichs also read parts of the book and added a valuable perspective from international relations. For their excellent research assistance I thank Alex Blenkinsopp, Abigail Bright, Lisa Gourd, and Ravinder Thukral. I am indebted to Gerhard Boomgaarden and Miranda Thirkettle at Routledge, Donna White, and the copyeditor, Sue Dickinson, who saw this book through to production. All the usual disclaimers apply.

I owe a larger debt to many wonderful colleagues around the world, who have sent me their work, generously read and criticized my own, for their insights, and in very many cases for their friendship. At the risk of significant omissions (but for fear the acknowledgements will be longer than the book), thanks are due to Katja Franko Aas, Didier Bigo, John Braithwaite, Simon Bronitt, Mark Brown, David Brown, David Cole, Adam Crawford, David Dixon, Markus Dubber, Antony Duff, Benoît Dupont, David Dyzenhaus, the late Richard Ericson, David Garland, Peter Grabosky, Oren Gross, Klaus Günther, Willem de Haan, Kevin Haggerty, Bernard Harcourt, Tim Hope, John Ip, Samuel Issacharoff, Heike Jung, Michael Kempa, John Kleinig, Nicola Lacey, Mike Levi, David Levi-Faur, David Lyon, Eugene McLaughlin, Gabriel Mythen, Mike Nellis, Tim Newburn, James Nickel, Pat O'Malley, Victor Ramraj, Peter Ramsay, Robert Reiner, Kent Roach, Sarah Percy, Clifford Shearing, Jonathan Simon, Victor Tadros, Adam Tomkins, Marianne Valverde, Andrew von Hirsch, Alison Wakefield, Leanne Webber, and Jennifer Wood. My thanks are also due to my graduate students for challenging my assumptions and introducing me to security in more guises than I could otherwise have imagined.

Earlier papers out of which this book evolved were given at seminars or conferences at the Australian National University (ANU), Canberra, and at the Universities of Cambridge, Birmingham, Edinburgh, Glasgow, the Humboldt Berlin, Leeds, Sheffield, LSBU London, Montreal, New South Wales (UNSW) Sydney, Oxford, Stirling, and at the British Academy, the University of Chicago Paris Center, and the Royal Netherlands Academy of Arts and Sciences, Amsterdam. I thank my hosts and all those who participated for their input and criticisms. I have also benefited enormously from the time spent over the years as Visiting Fellow at the Regulatory Institutions Network, ANU, Canberra, and at the Faculty of Law, UNSW Sydney.

As ever, the greatest debt is to Joshua and to our daughters Naomi and Esther for their love and support, and with apologies for the fact that they are now more security-conscious than they or I would like.

INTRODUCTION

Just a decade ago security had little claim to criminological attention. Security was the province of international relations, international law, and war studies. Security referred to national or military security, matters well beyond parochial criminological concerns. Today it is a central theme in criminology. Criminologists talk of 'governing security', 'governing through security', 'selling security', 'civilizing security', 'imagining security' and tackling 'insecurity', as well as making concrete reference to 'security management systems', 'private security', and the 'security industry'.[1]

The growth of security as a key subject of criminological analysis reflects the wider insecurity of twenty-first-century societies. The new obsession with security is a complex story that will be the task of this book to tell from the perspective of criminology. Much of the story derives from the growing importance of risk assessment and prudentialism whose coalescence in the 'new penology' or actuarial justice has signified a marked shift away from the largely retrospective orientation of the criminal justice process. Traditional, reactive strategies of crime control have been overlaid by prospective and preventive measures designed to maximize security. New techniques of crime prevention and community safety initiatives combine to render security a concern not only of the police but also of local authorities, inter-agency partnerships, voluntary groups, and private citizens. The burgeoning private security industry has generated a growing population of security agents ranging from individual operators, through medium-sized firms, to vast multinational security conglomerates employing tens, even hundreds, of thousands. In many jurisdictions private security personnel now outnumber those employed in public policing, such that the presumption of safety as a public good is being challenged by the notion of security as a private commodity. In both public and private spheres the pursuit of security is an enterprise in its own right with a dynamic and momentum distinct from crime rates. The consequence of these developments is that security is now a major object of public policy, of private enterprise, as well as hybrid public/private ventures. Together these factors explain why security now attracts so much criminological attention.

Beyond the domestic scene, transnational policing organizations and international associations have established a security terrain that traverses national boundaries, while commercial enterprise has created a global market for security. The attacks of 9/11 and the Bali, Madrid, and London bombings have kept security at the foreground of public concern. The so-called 'war on terror' has been driven by a desire to increase security in the face of catastrophic risk. Yet the exceptional powers justified by this purported state of emergency have grave implications for civil liberties and this has provoked intense political and academic debate about how and in what measure security should be pursued. The normalization of emergency powers, together with increased collaboration between policing and security and intelligence services, has eroded the distinction between security and crime control and blurred the already hazy line between public and private. These developments have also made urgently necessary a dispassionate analysis of what security is and what may justly be done in its name.

In short, a range of disciplinary paradigm shifts, policy changes, economic factors, and world political events have combined to shift security to the forefront of the criminological agenda. Security remains, however, too big an idea to be constrained by the disciplinary strictures of criminology, or indeed any other single discipline. The scholar of security must range not only over the disciplines of international relations, public international law, and war studies that have dominated the security field historically but also over political theory, legal philosophy, and economics. In these latter disciplines lies the possibility of thinking critically about security as a public good, as a means to other goods, and, most disturbingly, as a tradable commodity subject to the vagaries of the growing security market.

This book seeks to introduce, analyse, and criticize the concept of security in all its sundry forms and reflect upon its significance, implications, and dangers. It synthesizes the emergent criminological literature on security and situates this within debates about security occurring in other disciplines. Scholars have tended to think about security within their immediate discipline and in detachment from one another. One aim of this book, therefore, is to break down these boundaries in order better to understand security in all its variety and complexity.

To this end, Chapter 1 explores the multiple meanings condensed within the term security; meanings that lend it both appeal and ambiguous power (Zedner 2003a). Although security is the common currency of diverse academic disciplines it is used in strikingly different ways in each of them. Security is revealed as an objective policy goal, as subjective perception, as pursuit and practice, as symbolic assurance, and as a public good at the heart of the modern state. The chapter will consider security as an object of public policy, a subject of commercial venture by the private security industry, and as a means of governance (Valverde 2001).

Chapter 2 furnishes a brief history of security as an idea capable of rapid metamorphosis. It delineates the genealogy of security, examining classical writings on security that identify it with the emergence of the sovereign state, before going on to explore the emergence of the welfare state and the re-conceptualization of security as social security. Perhaps the dominant concept of security in the twentieth century has been that of national security, made central by two world wars and, in altered guise, also by the onset of the Cold War which brought national security concerns to the fore generated by international security and the development of 'security studies' as a distinct sub-discipline of international relations (Waever 1995, Krause and Williams 1997, Buzan, Waever *et al.* 1998, Wyn-Jones 1999). Of particular interest for criminology is the concept of human security. Though not uncontroversial, human security promotes a new focus on people rather than states and on security as residing in personal, communal, and environmental protection not only or chiefly in national or military security. In so doing it brings about a convergence between international relations and criminology – as criminology concerns itself with ever larger threats to security, so international relations finds its solution in the domestic and the mundane. One consequence is that security provides the lens through which more and more problems are viewed, a hazardous phenomenon neatly captured by the tag 'securitization'.

Chapter 3 seeks to map security by examining the contemporary political landscape, the dominance of economic rationality, and the place of security within it. In particular it explores the tensions that arise between the neoliberal imperative that security be a matter of private responsibility (manifest in prudential behaviour, the consumption of commercial security, and insurance products) and the role of the state as provider of security. This chapter seeks to chart the structural, political, and cultural changes that have altered security provision beyond recognition, in particular the erosion of the external/internal aspects of security, the complex arrangements set in place by the multiplication of security providers, and the impact of different political economies on the meaning and distribution of security.

Chapter 4 explores the relationship between security and criminal justice traditionally conceived. It examines changing conceptions of crime in the security society; how policing and criminal justice practices are transformed by the imperatives of security; and explores the continuing place of the 'post-crime' mechanisms of the traditional criminal process and punishment in what appears increasingly to be a 'pre-crime' society. It focuses in particular on the growth of surveillance, situational crime prevention, risk assessment and management, civil preventive measures, and the move from punishment to precaution as some of the more significant challenges security throws up for criminal justice (Ericson 2007).

Chapter 5 examines how the selling of security has produced a commodity available to those able and willing to pay yet denied to those without such means (Loader 1997a, 1999, Hope 2000). It examines what drives the burgeoning of the private security industry, how security has become a subject of commercial consumption, and a commodity to be traded in the emerging market for crime control. The goals of the private security industry and the economics of the security market throw up particular challenges for the protection of security as a public good. And yet the means of its regulation are, as yet, fragmentary and inadequate (Jones and Newburn 1998; Zedner 2006a). Beyond the local operations of security firms, the growth of transnational security provision, and, not least, the operation of private military companies in theatres of war, in conflict zones, and transitional democracies create newly urgent concerns about the consequences of commodifying security.

Chapter 6 examines how criminological understandings of security have been altered by the war on terror. Although counter-terrorism is framed by the language of states of exception and emergency powers, terrorism no longer stands outside the criminological lexicon, not least because exceptional or emergency security measures introduced ostensibly against terrorists have become normalized and their draconian powers applied against ordinary criminals. The high levels of uncertainty surrounding potentially catastrophic risks permit new more expansive measures against terrorist threats that undermine basic criminal justice principles. This chapter examines debates in philosophy and political theory about how to balance security and liberty in the fight against terror and how these deliberations, in turn, influence and inform criminological debates around security (Waldron 2003, 2006, Zedner 2005).

Finally, Chapter 7 examines the challenges and paradoxes thrown up by the pursuit of security and their implications for its governance. This chapter draws upon an emerging literature that enters a plea for uncertainty and an invitation to conceive risk as opportunity not threat (O'Malley 2004a; Ericson 2007). It considers the relationship between the means of seeking security and the ends which are sought by it. And it focuses in particular on the relationship between security and changes in the shape and role of the modern state, as one player in a mixed market of security provision. The values that ought to inform the pursuit of security lie at the heart of contemporary governance and this chapter explores contentious current debates about its meaning and place (Shearing and Wood 2003a, 2003b, Hudson 2003, Loader and Walker 2004). More controversial still is the proposition that security itself has become a means by which states govern, and the chapter examines whether we are now governed 'through security' (Simon 1997, Valverde 2001). Attempting to reassert security as a public good and as the very means to the good society is suggested as one way of seeking to avoid the danger that security becomes a prison of our own making. The book concludes by trying to set out some starting principles by which to govern security and to delimit what otherwise appears as its insatiable lure.

In sum, this book addresses security, its place in contemporary crime control, and the means to its governance. In order to grasp just how far crime control has changed to render security so central a matter of contemporary concern we need a rough guide or map. This book explains why security has come to such prominence; offers a guide to the sprawling literature on security; and provides a timely critical reflection on the concept and its relationship to the central themes of contemporary criminology. In so doing it seeks to give some concrete meaning to the idea of security and to circumscribe its limits by providing an account of what security is (and what it is not).

The developments described in this book are disparate and not easily amenable to coherent explanation. Superficially there appears to be little in common between the burglar alarm and the satellite tracking system or the work of the bouncer and the security systems analyst. But is there an underlying logic common to them all – the logic of security perhaps? Given the speed with which the discourse of security has taken hold of the criminological imagination, this book offers the reader the opportunity to survey the field and to make sense of the many and varied meanings of this inherently complex and powerful idea.

1

THE SEMANTICS OF SECURITY

Security is a promiscuous concept. It is wantonly deployed
in fields as diverse as social security, health and safety,
financial security, policing and community safety, national
security, military security, human security, environmental
security, international relations and peacekeeping. For security to keep such varied bedfellows as these, it must be not
only promiscuous but also inconstant, appearing as different
objects of desire in different places and at different times.
Yet security wears these multiple identities so lightly it is
easy to overlook the fact that it is not a single, immutable
concept but many. As Valverde has observed: '[t]he abstract
noun "security" is an umbrella term that both enables and
conceals a very diverse array of governing practices, budget-
ary practices, political and legal practices, and social and
cultural values and habits' (Valverde 2001: 90).

Once primarily the domain of international relations,
political science, public international law, and military studies (for an overview of this literature, see Kolodziej 2005),
security was traditionally conceived as the defence of the
sovereign state against external threat. It remains a central
concept in war studies and international relations but it has

developed new usages and meanings in many other fields: finance, economics, health, and development studies being among the most prominent. Only relatively recently has it become a prominent theme in criminological literature (for example, Dupont and Wood 2006, Jones 2007, Loader and Walker 2007, Wood and Shearing 2007).

Security is now changing the very nature of criminological endeavour and eroding important criminological categories and presumptions. Previously clear-cut distinctions between policing and security services, between crime and terrorism, between domestic and national security, between community safety and international peacekeeping are being blurred. The embryonic dialogue consequently emerging with international relations is but the latest iteration of a long history of interaction with and borrowing from other disciplines. The study of security is increasingly characterized by convergence and cross-fertilization, generating in turn a new corpus of transdisciplinary security scholarship. It follows that although the focus of this book is on its usages in contemporary crime control and policing, security cannot properly be understood other than within the context of larger debates. In short, security is too big an idea to be constrained by the strictures of any single discipline.

Linguistically, security is a slippery and contested term that conveys many meanings and has many referent objects, ranging from the individual to the state to the biosphere. Notwithstanding its inherent imprecision, or perhaps because of it, security has gained considerable prominence across disparate policy fields. Its lack of definitional clarity permits expansive interpretation and wide application. The resultant ambiguity about what is promised, provided, sold, or sought when security is invoked is a form of licence. It allows the sellers of security to peddle their wares without specifying what exactly is on offer and consumers to buy into security policies or products for quite different reasons without needing to articulate or reconcile their differences (Loader 1999). Imprecision allows diverse measures and policies to be justified in the name of security. Little wonder then that the capaciousness of security has been recognized by politicians as a lever to attract votes and augment state power, as well as by salesmen as a means to boost consumption of security products and services.

Security is often deployed in universalist terms that pay little attention to the ways in which it is articulated, understood, and pursued in different legal cultures. Superficial similarities in terminology (*security, sécurité, Sicherheit*) mask widely varying usages across jurisdictions deriving from differences in local history, social structure, and legal and political cultures. It is not enough to observe the different meanings given to security in different languages: the institutions and practices that make up the lives of security need to be studied too. Significant differences in perceptions and tolerance of threats, ordering practices, and patterns of social cohesion shape local perceptions of security (and insecurity) and dictate how it is mobilized politically. Security varies in its importance; in its location between state, private, and civil society; and, not least, in its very meaning even within that supposedly homogenous entity that is Europe. Universalizing claims about the convergence of crime control practices under conditions of late modernity (Garland 2001) does not withstand comparative analysis of the varieties of local culture, organization, and distribution of security between, and even within, nation states (Sparks 2001, Newburn 2006). For example, although poverty as a threat to security may have been displaced by terrorism in most Western jurisdictions, in developing countries it remains a primary source of insecurity. It follows that security is also an idea ripe for comparative analysis in order to establish the varied meanings that attach depending on location and context (Zedner 2003a).

The prominence of security in contemporary society is most obviously explained by reference to the extraneous threats that have recently provided the very justification for security laws, policies, measures, services, and products. The events of 9/11, subsequent terrorist atrocities, the threat of guns, drugs, international serious and organized crime (to say nothing of military conflicts, genocide, pandemics, and environmental disasters) license extraordinary and exceptional measures; the suspension of normal rules and procedures; derogation from rights and principles; and even states of emergency (Ackerman 2004, Tribe and Gudridge 2004, Agamben 2004). In the name of security, things that would ordinarily be politically untenable become thinkable. As Freedman observes: 'censorship can be imposed, political rights suspended, young men conscripted, and aliens deported all in the name of security' (Freedman 2003: 752). The pursuit of security signals an urgency and importance that stifles debate as to priorities, resources, and countervailing interests. To invoke security is a move to foreclose debate as to the wisdom of a policy or the necessity of a measure. In short, security has all the qualities of a fire engine, replete with clanging bells and flashing lights, whose dash to avert imminent catastrophe brooks no challenge, even if it risks running people down on the way to the fire.

But without clarity the concept remains unwieldy, scarcely capable of rational analysis. Precision not only is conceptually and analytically important; it also serves as a restraint on the claims that can be made in the name of security. It is for these reasons that this book adopts a deliberately cool, dispassionate look at what it means to invoke security. This is all the more important at a time when, in addition to justifying public policy, security is being marketed as a valuable commodity. Security is produced by private security firms, sold and traded commercially, and enjoyed as a club good available only by those who buy access or rights to it (Crawford 2006b). Even in the public sector 'security' has become akin to an industry and public officials, quite as much as their commercial counterparts, seek profit in selling security policies and solutions. Its antonym 'insecurity' drives crime control, policing, anti-terrorism policies, and corporate security production and is largely responsible for the rise of 'reassurance policing' and community safety programmes, as well as the proliferation of security hardware, services, and technologies (Zedner 2008a). More recently, 'security' has been invoked adjectivally to describe the forms of relations by which it is distributed – hence 'security assemblage', 'security net-works', 'security nodes', 'security quilts', and 'security bubbles' (all of which will be analysed further in Chapter 3). Finally, its derivative 'securitization' denotes the, generally adverse, ethical and analytical consequences of structuring diverse policy issues in terms of security (Waever 1995). Securitization recognizes that it is not only an analytical category but also a category of practice or 'speech act', a way of framing and responding to social problems.

The applications of security in the public and private spheres span the end goals of objective safety from threat; the subjective condition of feeling secure; and the assurance or guarantee thereof. In these different guises, security carries a normative meaning as a public good that must be defended by the state (Loader and Walker 2007). Because security in either objective or subjective guises can rarely be said to be attained, the word 'pursuit', be it of national, military, public, community or personal safety, perhaps better describes the ongoing venture that is security. Finally, security has a symbolic quality which varies by, and within, jurisdictions, as well as over time. It is the product of local conditions and local understandings of what threatens and how best to protect against it. These meanings of security – objective, subjective, pursuit, practice, and symbol – will be the subject of the remainder of this chapter.

SECURITY AS OBJECTIVE STATE

The state of security refers to two quite distinct objective and subjective conditions. The objective state of absolute security implies a condition of being without threat, which, even if it could be achieved today, always remains liable to negation by new threats tomorrow. Although we may aspire to the state of security, it makes sense to recognize that its perfect attainment is unachievable, not least since security is predicated on the continuing presence of that which threatens it. Understood this way, security is the condition of 'being protected from threats' – whether through their neutralization, through avoidance, or through non-exposure to risk. Advertence to threats implies a temporal quality to security: it persists only in as much as and for so long as threats are annulled or avoided. As Valverde observes, it is a political and grammatical fallacy 'to mistake "security" for a concrete noun':

> 'Security' is not something we can have more of or less of, because it is not a thing at all. It is . . . the name we use for a temporally extended state of affairs characterized by the calculability and predictability of the future.
>
> (Valverde 2001: 85)

Others take a less sceptical position, viewing security as a concrete and necessary precondition to human flourishing. Shue, for example, argues:

> No one can fully enjoy any right that is supposedly protected by society if someone can credibly threaten him or her with murder, rape, beating, etc., when he or she tries to enjoy the alleged

right. Such threats to physical security are among the most serious and – in much of the world – the most widespread hindrances to the enjoyment of any right. If any right is to be exercised except at great risk, physical security must be protected.

(Shue 1996: 21)

Even in its objective condition, security may take more or less concrete forms. While Shue perceives objective security as protection against physical harm, Wolfers, for example, took the view that 'security, in any objective sense, measures the absence of threats to acquired values' (Buzan 1991: 17, Lustgarten and Leigh 1994: ch. 1). The physical and political aspects of objective security are often related: that which threatens physically commonly also poses a threat to values or the stability of a political system. But there is no necessary relation between the two. For example, the threat posed by terrorists to the political regime and its core values may far outweigh the physical harm posed to its citizens – a fact recognized by those terrorist groups that give warnings prior to attack.

Substantively then, objective security is defined by reference to that which is deemed to be a threat: financial security defends against theft and deception, military security against armed conflict, and the newly coined 'homeland' security is generally defined by reference to terrorism. Security is at once both contextual and relational: its attainment measured by how far policies succeed in reducing or eliminating the particular threat against which they are intended to ward. A lot of hidden work is being done by the supposed peril against which security guards and the very idea of threat can usefully be unpacked. Arguably the real impossibility of objective security is a function of the fact that threats are, at least in part, subjective constructs. Something is regarded as a threat to be secured against only if it raises the prospect of depriving someone of something that they value. Given that any individual's understanding of value is subjective and constantly changing, what is considered a threat is also constantly in flux and it follows that objective security is arguably less readily distinguishable from the subjective state than at first appears.

SECURITY AS SUBJECTIVE STATE

Security is also used to refer to a second state, namely the subjective sense we have of our own safety. In this second sense, security is all in the mind: though of course our subjective sense of safety derives in part from material and social conditions. The subjective state of security as tranquillity or freedom from care has long historic roots that are traceable to the Latin *securitas* and the German *Sicherheitsgefühl*, both of which denote the feeling of being secure (Rothschild 1995: 61). Subjective security can take the form of either the absolute condition of feeling safe or, more usually, a qualified condition of freedom from anxiety or apprehension because feelings of insecurity have been allayed. Here both 'security' and its antonym 'insecurity' refer to an existential state that varies not only according to objective risk but also according to extraneous factors such as individual sensitivity to risk and danger.

Subjective security may be correlated with objective security but may equally be quite unrelated to the level of objective threat faced. For example, young men often remain fearless despite the fact that statistically they are most at risk from assault, whereas women and the elderly may modify or curtail their movements outside the home despite the lower statistical likelihood of their being victims of violent assault (Hoyle and Zedner 2007: 465–6). This is not to say that the insecurities suffered by the latter group are irrational. Although the likelihood of an attack is lower, its consequences may be considerably greater for a vulnerable victim's ontological sense of safety. Less readily rationalized is the fact that perceptions of security threats are often quite unrelated to risk. Fear of flying persists despite the evidence that the risks of road travel are much greater than those posed by air transport. Note that an American study found that the probability of being killed in one non-stop airline flight 'is about one in 13 million (even taking the 11 September crashes into account), while to reach that same level of risk when driving on America's safest roads, rural interstate highways, one would have to travel a mere 11.2 miles'.[1]

The important point is that subjective insecurity has a life related to but not necessarily closely correlated with object-ive risk and that failure by governments to take seriously concerns that are genuinely held only exacerbates this sense of vulnerability. As Pavarini has observed of Italy:

> The growing social demand for security against crime reflects subjective feelings of insecurity, regardless of whether this sense of insecurity is or is not well founded and the results of an objective state of diminished security. This growing demand for security manifests itself as a protest against the institutional and public offerings of social defence. Institutional and public efforts to provide safeguards against criminality are perceived as being unable to meet the social demand for security.
>
> (Pavarini 1997: 79)

Security in this subjective sense is better captured by the German concept of *Innere Sicherheit*, which makes more explicit reference to the psychological costs of insecurity than does its English-language counterpart. Bauman observes that the German term *Sicherheit* embraces three distinct ideas: security, certainty, and safety (though we might question just how distinct these ideas are in English).

This, he argues, renders security open to a particularly powerful form of political exploitation:

> In an ever more insecure and uncertain world the withdrawal into the safe haven of territoriality is an intense temptation. . . . It is perhaps a happy coincidence for political operators and hopefuls that the genuine problems of insecurity and uncertainty have condensed into the anxiety about safety: politicians can be supposed to be doing something about the first two just because being seen to be vociferous and vigorous about the third.
>
> (Bauman 1998: 117)

The political capital inherent in subjective security derives also from the fact that expressions of insecurity about crime serve, in Taylor's words, as 'a convenient and socially-approved kind of metaphor through which survey respondents can articulate, in shorthand fashion, a much more complex sense of restlessness and anxiety – not least the general unease which a full-blown free market environment produces culturally and psychologically' (Taylor 1998: 23). If Taylor is right, then it would be a mistake to expect feelings of insecurity to correlate in any direct way with levels of recorded crime since they may encapsulate a much larger set of concerns, coalescing perhaps around security of the environment, of health, employment, and the economy.

Like objective security, subjective security has a marked temporal quality. It is enjoyed only so long as the individual is persuaded that the protection he or she enjoys or the evasive action he or she has taken suffices to ward off threats. The vulnerability of subjective security to awareness of new sources of threat renders its attainment transient and its scope inherently expansive. Freedman has observed: 'Once anything that generates anxiety or threatens the quality of life in some respect becomes labelled as a "security problem" the field risks losing all focus' (Freedman 1998: 53).

Analytically therefore, subjective security is hazardous: it may mean almost anything anyone chooses. Normatively, the danger is that, widely cast, subjective security and, in particular, the need to assuage public insecurities become a justification for measures that may have adverse consequences for that minority of the population that must bear the brunt of them and which does little to improve conditions of objective security for the majority. A challenge, to which we will return below, is how to maximize subjective security at least cost to individual liberties and to unpopular minorities.

SECURITY AS PURSUIT

Conceiving of security as a pursuit rather than as an end goal means recognizing that it is probably unattainable and at best impermanent (Zedner 2000). An inherently relational concept (Freedman 2003), security must endlessly be tested against threats as yet unknown. The vulnerability or inadequacies of its provision are revealed only if and when those threats eventuate. Security must therefore be continually revised in the light of the latest challenge to its attainment, necessarily imperfect assessments of likely future threats, and its vulnerability to them.

Conceiving security as a pursuit also better fits its common usage across disparate spheres and does not tie security to any single referent object. National security, military security, and community safety can all sensibly be described as exercises in the pursuit of security without relying on this single word to capture the considerable differences in their scope, scale, and focus of operations. In each case security is a reference to a cluster of ongoing policies and practices which, like talk of security budgets, imply a continuing investment and little expectation that security, in its objective sense, will one day be realized. In many Western jurisdictions it was precisely the growing acceptance that crime is a 'normal, commonplace, aspect of modern society' (Garland 2001: 128) that shifted interest from strategies of crime control and reduction to those of security and community safety. Declining faith in rehabilitation and deterrence has meant that the goal of crime reduction has been at least partially displaced by the pursuit of security against enduring threats.

Given the considerable political and financial capital invested in security, it may not be too cynical to contend that, even if it were attainable, absolute security is not a state actually sought either by politicians or by the captains of private security corporations. In both public and private spheres, security is an industry whose continued flourishing is predicated upon the persistence of insecurities. Happily for its promoters, security threats are not easily eradicable. The apparent inevitability of continuing crime, terrorism, and other security threats underwrites the security industry and serves as an incentive for further investment.

Ironically, even where the pursuit of security succeeds in diminishing risks (for example, by reducing crime), a collateral effect of security policies and services is to foster awareness of threats and stimulate those insecurities that underpin continuing demand for the products of the security industry. Security providers, reliant on demand for their products, have no interest in minimizing this effect: quite the contrary. While it would be unduly cynical to charge politicians with deliberately manufacturing fear of crime or overstating the threat of terrorism in order to serve ulterior political ends, the political capital in security has clearly not escaped their notice. Victory is always in the future. When one security threat is brought under control, another must be sought if it does not arise naturally. So it was that, in the context of declining crime rates and the relative political stability of the post-Cold War era, 9/11 provided a new *raison d'être* for police and security services.

In this sense security can also be considered as a 'practice'. Although this category overlaps to some degree with pursuit, it captures the fact it is the role and function of a wide range of practitioners: police, state security agents, private security guards, security managers, and security consultants whose work centres on defining the sources of (in)security as well as the techniques and technologies through which to manage them. The 'security field' is one of competing practitioners each peddling their wares, services, and solutions to myriad different security problems. Their professional discourses and methodologies have only begun to attract the attention of security scholars but are essential to understanding how security is constructed and plied not only in pursuit of an end goal but as a continuing activity (Bigo 2001: 98).

SECURITY AS SYMBOL

Material conceptions of security reside in tangible efforts to pursue or attain objective security by reducing risk and improving safety, whether through concrete measures, physical devices, or working practices. Altogether less tangible is the symbolic life of security. Although symbolic security is more amorphous, it may speak directly to ontological insecurities and can be effective in assuaging insecurity and positively enhancing subjective feelings of security. As Loader astutely observes, 'Security . . . has become the ideology of the post-ideological age; absolute safety the utopian hankering of a world that is supposed to have lost interest in utopias' (Loader 2008: 404).

Security is rhetorically powerful and has a strong emotional appeal that arises in no small part from its capacity to bear multiple meanings simultaneously. The rhetorical allure of security has seen it attached to a long line of neologisms (global security, international security, cooperative security, and human security) that deliberately use the term to mobilize political support and economic resources (Valverde 2001: 85). Security as rhetoric resides in the promises made by politicians to tackle threats to personal or communal safety and in the slogans and advertising campaigns of commercial security firms. Symbolic security underpins the promotion of neighbourhood watch and community safety stickers by local police; the security marking of bicycles, car radios, and other valuables; and the security posters that adorn airports, railway stations, and other places of perceived high risk. Although these offerings can rarely be shown to have any direct impact on risk reduction, they may play a reassurance function, persuading constituents and consumers that their concerns are being taken seriously and offering at least a sticking plaster of protection.

A more cynical reading of the symbolic role of security is found in the concept of 'security theater' (Schneier 2006: 38). Security theatre refers to largely palliative measures introduced in the name of security but taken primarily to allay public fears or at least persuade them that something is being done. Examples include many of the measures taken in airports in respect of departing passengers, for example, the requirement that gels and liquids be carried in small quantities only and in clear plastic bags. Others include automatically opening gates on residential roads and tamper-proof packaging on foods (ibid.). A more dramatic example of security theatre arose in February 2003 when, on the basis of intelligence that Al-Qaeda would mount an attack with surface-to-air missiles on London's Heathrow airport, the government deployed armoured tanks, a Nimrod MR2 reconnaissance aircraft, and 1,500 armed police and troops to patrol in and around the airport.[2] Although ostensibly based upon credible intelligence of a planned 'spectacular' attack, sceptics suggested that the decision to turn the airport into a quasi-military zone was less to do with an imminent threat and more about seeking to persuade the growing number opposed to the war with Iraq of its necessity: 'After all, it was argued, tanks would be of little practical value to anyone – other than their occupants – in the event of a missile attack on the airport.' Highly visible demonstrations of state commitment to counter feared threats may have little or no practical effect in increasing objective security but seek to satisfy public demand for reassurance; silence critics; or, as in this particular case, serve to legitimize military action in the face of public opposition.

Viewed positively, security theatre may indeed meet legitimate concerns about subjective insecurity, especially where the perception of threat is a greater problem than the threat itself. Insofar as it provides reassurance, it may even prove part of the solution. For example, persuading people that it is safe to travel on public transport or go out at night may actually reduce risks by increasing natural surveillance. Security theatre may also have some marginal effect in deterring the poorly informed. For example, fake speed cameras, mock in-store surveillance cameras, and signs warning of security patrols may reduce speeding, shoplifting and other property crimes. Whether CCTV footage is actually observed or a factory is patrolled by guards and ferocious dogs may matter less than the fact that the public believe themselves to be watched or a building to be guarded. Provided the appearance given is sufficient to deter there is no need, indeed no justification, for material measures.

On the other hand, since symbolic security is rarely cost-less, it may operate to the detriment of more efficacious but less publicly visible measures from which resources are consequently diverted. Moreover, security theatre may erode civil liberties by burdening suspect populations with conspicuous measures taken against them without warrant. In seeking to assuage public concerns it may pander to irrational fears instead of educating the public about the real levels of risk (Roberts 2005). Ironically, by providing visible reminders of the risks it purports to address, security theatre may even exacerbate existing fears. An extreme example occurred in America when elementary school children in Tennessee were terrified by teachers who staged a fictitious gun attack during a class trip (telling them it was not a drill) in the name of providing a 'learning experience'.[3] Even everyday security measures such as burglar and car alarms have the capacity to generate insecurity in those obliged to use them. More common still is the manufacture of security services and products by companies that are keen to maximize profits by exploiting insecurity. An unquantifiable share of the private security market is taken up by services and products that do little more than provide assurance. As the President of US security firm Westec energetically affirmed: 'we are not a security guard company: We sell a *concept* of security' (quoted in Davis 1990: 250). This self-conscious recognition by the purveyors of security that what they sell is something other than physical protection against threat was delivered apparently without irony or apology.

CONCLUSION

This chapter has outlined just some of the ways in which the concept of security is deployed. These range from objectively measurable, if impermanent, levels of 'securedness' and subjective feelings of safety, through security as pursuit or practice, to the more ephemeral manifestations of security as symbol, rhetoric, and theatre. Of course it is debatable whether these distinctions between objective and subjective security and between symbolic and instrumental measures can always be clearly drawn. While analytically useful, in practice they are often a good deal less clear than this. In the following chapters the complex and inconstant quality of security will become even more apparent as we go on to look at the genealogy, distribution, and different substantive applications of security across the fields of criminal justice, the private security industry, and counter-terrorism. In each of these fields security presents itself in a new guise, its meaning altering according to time, place, and context. This inconstancy might matter less were it not for the power that resides in ambiguity. No small part of the lure of security is that the variety of these guises makes it possible to appeal to the idea in pursuit of multiple different objectives and in respect of policies that might otherwise appear indefensible. It follows that pinning security down is not only analytically important but it has important political and policy implications too.

2

A BRIEF HISTORY OF SECURITY

In order to explain how the concept of security came to influence so many fields let us trace the genealogy of its modern usage. This genealogy is not just a matter of academic interest, for whereas many concepts change beyond recognition over time, the historical meanings of security are not so much sequential as cumulative. Over the course of the last several hundred years, security has acquired layers of meaning that have lost little of their relevance today – with the result that the writings of Hobbes, Locke, Smith, Bentham, and Mill speak to us as clearly now as when they were written. Charting the shifting interpretations and changing applications of security historically is essential therefore to understanding the multiple strata of ideas still embedded in this single term.

CLASSICAL WRITINGS ON SECURITY

The birth of the modern concept of security can be traced to the seventeenth century, when it was articulated most fully in the writings of Thomas Hobbes. Hobbes argued that without security, man remains in the 'state of nature', which is a 'dissolute condition of masterlesse men, without subjection to Lawes, and a coercive Power to tye their hands from rapine, and revenge' (Hobbes 1651: ch. 18). In this dismal condition, 'men live without other security, than what their own strength, and their own invention shall furnish them'. If life is not to be, in Hobbes' now famous phrase, 'solitary, poore, nasty, brutish, and short', obedience to the sovereign as a contract and not a condition for membership of society is essential. The mutual covenant to obey a common authority or sovereign power is the basis for political society and the only means by which to guarantee security.

The Hobbesian conception of security was powerfully challenged by John Locke's insight that liberty is best served not by absolute state power but by a system of checks and balances furnished by the separation of legislature, executive, and judiciary (Locke 1690). Thus modified, securing liberty provided the *raison d'être* of the emergent modern state. For Locke, civil society was formed for the purpose of protecting 'life, liberty, and estate'. Re-reading Locke through the lens of present concerns, Neocleous argues that property serves as shorthand for protected interests and understood this way security becomes the foundation for market society. Accordingly, although Locke is commonly thought of as an author of modern liberalism, Neocleous suggests that he 'might in fact be thought to inaugurate less a tradition of "liberty" and much more a *liberal* discourse on the *priority of security*' (Neocleous 2008: 14). On this conception, security limited the role of the state to providing the conditions for a free market and upholding private property rights.

This reformulation of security as the necessary precondition of liberty was further developed in the writings of political theorists Jeremy Bentham and John Stuart Mill. Bentham elaborated a 'security-providing principle' that set security as the most important object of legislative policy and the primary source of utility. Indeed, he described the 'care of security' as the 'principal object of the Laws' (Bentham 1843: 308). Bentham did not value liberty for its own sake and equated pure liberty with the absence of government and law. For Bentham 'liberty' was an emotive term, the use of which in politics distracted attention from the fact that it was essentially by restrictions on freedom that happiness was made possible. Yet his definition of security was very close to what we might think of as liberty: namely a secure framework in which to form and pursue one's interests without interference from others, whether this be personal security against injury by others or political security against intrusions by state authority (Dinwiddy 1978: 21).

Bentham's formulation of security as providing certainty of expectation thus emphasized the need to minimize contingency and maximize predictability so that choices made today might be fulfilled tomorrow. In so doing Bentham distinguished between different types of utility – original and expectation utilities, or those grounded in nature and those grounded on expectations. Expectation utilities depend upon projecting the individual into the future and are derived from the prospect of being able to achieve a future benefit. Bentham uses expectation to refer to beliefs based on a system of rules such that expectation utilities are those derived from rule systems. The higher degree of certainty provided, the greater the expectation and hence the greater the utility derived from it. If one sees security as equivalent to certainty of expectation then minimizing contingency is intimately related to well-being.

Understood this way, the distinction between liberty and security begins to diminish since liberty can be exercised and choices made on a rational basis only in the context of a pattern of secured expectation. If one accepts that the institutions of law are the primary means of minimizing the influence of contingency then stable patterns of expectation are reliant upon an authoritative system of rules. Security is the means by which expectation utilities can be established and maintained (Kelly 1990: 77). As Bentham put it: 'the idea of his security must be prolonged to him throughout the whole vista that his imagination can measure' (Bentham 1843: 308). Implicit in this is the assumption that security of expectation is a structural precondition for the formation of interests and desires. Security is thus necessarily future-orientated or, as Bentham put it: 'security turns its eye exclusively to the future' (Kelly 1990: quoted 77). Security here is a necessary precondition of liberty because only when secure can an individual formulate goals and make decisions about the future in the expectation that they will be realized.

Mill also regarded liberty and security as closely connected: in his writing security is a necessary precondition to freedom of action and, simultaneously, the only ground upon which liberty can justifiably be eroded. According to Mill, 'the sole end for which mankind are warranted, individually or collectively, in interfering with the liberty of action of any of their number, is self-protection' (Mill 1979: 13). Mill posited security as 'the most vital of all interests', insisting that 'security of person and property . . . are the first needs of society' on the grounds that 'security no human being can possibly do without; on it we depend for all our immunity from evil, and for the whole value of all and every good, beyond the passing moment; since nothing but the gratification of the instant could be of any worth to us, if we could be deprived of anything the next instant by whoever was momentarily stronger than ourselves' (Mill 1972: 50). For liberalism, security came to refer to the liberty of secure possessions, while government existed principally for the protection of property. The development of the police in the nineteenth century can therefore be read as a means of securing the interests of the propertied against those without, and thus of fabricating and maintaining a particular form of social order (Neocleous 2000b).

The idea of security as intimately related with liberty came to be widely accepted in the liberal tradition. As Burchell observes, by 'the end of the eighteenth century the terms liberty and security have become almost synonymous' (Burchell 1991: 139). Late eighteenth- and early nineteenth-century conceptions of security posited an established and settled government whose role it was to provide the conditions for a free society by fostering economic independence and individual self-reliance. Highly influential were the earlier ideas of Adam Smith:

> it is not so much the regulations of the police which preserves the security of a nation as the custom of having in it as few servants and dependants as possible. Nothing tends so much to corrupt and enervate and debase the mind as dependency, and nothing gives such noble and generous notions of probity as freedom and independency. Commerce is one great preventive of this custom.
>
> (Smith 1978 [1762]: 333)

At the core of this minimalist conception of the state was the establishment of a formal police set up to further the preventive function of protecting property (though resisted at the time by propertied classes, who did not relish bearing the financial burdens this would entail). This conception of policing differed significantly from that of the modern police as adjuncts to a penal system of prosecution and punishment. The vocabularies of 'preventive justice', of 'social prophylaxis', and of the 'preventive police' (Chadwick 1829) make clear how security through prevention was preferred over retrospective prosecution and punishment. Hence the observation by Blackstone that: '*Preventive* justice is upon every principle of reason, of humanity, and of sound policy, preferable in all respects to *punishing* justice.'[1]

Running in parallel to these distinctly Anglo-Saxon conceptions of security, very different historical ideas about police and police science developed in continental Europe. In the German tradition, for example, the concept of *Polizei* combined three distinct notions: the condition of order in the community or the prerequisites to good order; laws whose object was the establishment and maintenance of good order; and finally, a more narrowly defined reference to the contents of specific rules or legislation pertaining to 'police matters' or the regulation of conduct tending to disorder. To these early concepts of police was added a theological literature of 'the order of estates' or the necessary foundations for a well-regulated community (Kneymeyer 1980: 179). *Polizeiwissenschaft* or police science concerned not only the condition of communal order but also the means to be deployed in order to achieve it. This encompassed quite a different set of understandings about the meaning of order and the institutions necessary to its realization. Although its meaning and the means to achieve it varied by jurisdiction, it is clear that security – in the larger sense of governmentality – became a common feature and defining purpose of the rise of the modern state (Foucault 2007).[2]

Despite the commitment of political theorists to security through prevention, the establishment of prisons, reformatories, asylums, and workhouses in the nineteenth century delivered an altogether more reactive, disciplinary mode of security based upon exclusion, incarceration, and isolation (Rothman 1971, Ignatieff 1978, Foucault 1979). According to Foucault, these institutions were intended not only to provide security against those they contained (the criminal, the insane, the inebriate, and impoverished or 'dangerous' classes, as they were called) but also to act as mechanisms of discipline throughout wider society. Prisons, in particular, have been identified as a means of controlling the working classes or a source of labour discipline essential to emergent capitalism (Melossi and Pavarini 1981) and at the heart of a larger complex or 'carceral archipelago' (Foucault 1979: 297) of disciplinary institutions. 'Is it surprising', Foucault asks, 'that prisons resemble factories, schools, barracks, hospitals, which all resemble prisons?' (Foucault 1979: 228).

The classic problem of industrialization was that it created a surplus and therefore potentially dangerous population. According to Christie's account, prisons, reformatories, and workhouses together formed a 'crime-control industry' devoted to resolving this potential threat to good order by incarcerating the surplus population in ever-increasing numbers (Christie 1994). Subjecting their inmates to a regime of surveillance, 'normalization', and discipline, these institutions sought to create 'docile bodies' that would no longer pose a threat to the good order of society (Foucault 1979: 135ff). They also provided strong prudential reasons for self-discipline, restraint, and conformity among the working poor, who were anxious to remain outside their walls. Equally during industrialization in America, powerful industrial elites used their own systems of surveillance, social control, and discipline over workers both inside and outside the walls of factories. For example, the Ford Motor Company had various strategies for worker control, not least employing private detectives to 'provide a disciplined supply of labour to power capitalist industrialization' (Weiss 1986: 87). Arguably this presents an overly deterministic account of the relationship between economic change and structural developments in security provision, but it nonetheless captures an important aspect of security as fundamental to the development of industry, commerce, and prosperity (and also of security as industry itself), to which we will return in Chapter 5.

For all that the nineteenth century in Britain is synonymous with laissez-faire and the minimal state, elsewhere – Bismarck's Germany is an obvious example – state building moved apace. It was during this period that many of the 'apparatuses of security' at the heart of the modern state were established (Foucault 1991: 104). In addition to the carceral institutions already described, formal police forces were set up and increasingly deemed essential to the maintenance of security and the good order of what became known as 'civil society'. Likewise the state's growing military machine and expanding diplomatic offices were regarded as essential guarantors of national security against external military attack, particularly during the Napoleonic Wars and in the period after.

This burgeoning of state power at the very time when laissez-faire was supposedly the dominant ideology can partly be explained by the perceived need to create the conditions in which market economics could flourish. A necessary condition of the state's security was prosperity, and this prosperity could not be guaranteed other than through policing, broadly defined. The indigent and unruly threatened the security of the state, of property, and of prosperity, and the role of the emergent police was to minimize this threat. Regulation of the poor, of vagrants and beggars, of gambling, and of alcohol consumption can all be seen as larger exercises in the police power (Dubber 2005, Dubber and Valverde 2006). In this sense the formation of state police was inseparable from the establishment of social security – both projects were aimed not merely at preventing crime but also at the positive fabrication of social order (Neocleous 2000b). As Neocleous has observed, 'social security can be seen as a form of policing, but conversely, policing might be read as the project of *social security*' (Neocleous 2007a: 36).

SOCIAL SECURITY AND THE WELFARE STATE

Individualism and self-reliance remained central tenets of political economy, in many Western jurisdictions in the later nineteenth century. There was, however, increasing disquiet about the ability of the market to provide economic security. Developing urbanization and increased mobility led to decline of local provision and kinship support and ushered in a new commitment to 'social security' delivered through a burgeoning apparatus of social administration designed to combat poverty, sickness, and to provide for education, sanitation, and housing. In part this political shift towards social security was made possible by the development of social statistics. Statistics provided the data with which to identify hazards, assess risk, and, thereby, to seek to tame chance (Hacking 1990, O'Malley 2004a: ch. 2). They thus provided the foundations of actuarial calculation, insurance, and what was to become a vast system for the collective identification and management of risk. The birth of what ultimately became known as the welfare state brought in a new and massively expanded role for government: that of providing social security for citizens through a complex system of taxation, social insurance, and redistributive policies designed to provide a safety net at vulnerable points in the life cycle (most obviously childhood, periods of ill-health, poverty, unemployment, and old age) (Titmuss 1958, Garland 1985: 40ff). Social security thus shifted the focus of security from protection against imminent hazards towards insurance against abstract and categorical future risks.

Although these new programmes of social security provided a minimum standard of living and a safety net for much of the population, security was not extended to all. Access to social security was limited to disciplined and willing workers who were able to contribute to the insurance regimes for ill-health, old age, and burial.[3] Would-be recipients of social security were required to display independence and self-discipline. Those deemed unemployable or 'degenerate' were excluded from the security of insurance schemes and instead shunted into workhouses, labour colonies, reformatories and prisons (Garland 1985: ch. 5). Social security thus maintained a decidedly disciplinary aspect, compelling prudent and responsible behaviour in those who would be recipients of its largesse, and subjecting to decidedly more rigorous penal discipline those deemed irresponsible. Only with the formation of a much expanded welfare state after the Second World War were social security and welfare adopted as matters of general right and universal access became a core principle, if not invariably a practice, of social security.

The development of social security in the late nineteenth and twentieth centuries was prompted in large part by domestic politics, not least the perceived need to meet and in so doing quell the demands of an increasingly powerful working class. In interwar America, for example, Roosevelt's New Deal was prompted as much by fear of political insurgence and the threat of communism as by the desperate poverty that accompanied the Great Depression. However, in many countries the consolidation of social security was prompted also by concern over the military security of the nation against external threat (Tilly 1985) and, in respect of European colonial powers, by the requirements of empire. The need for a physically fit population capable of military service and the defence of imperial interests was a major motivating factor behind the bid to tackle unemployment, low wages, poor housing, malnutrition, and other chronic health problems (Semmel 1960, Searle 1971). Social security was therefore deeply implicated in national security – a fact that was brought into sharp relief by the two world wars, which urgently required fit, well-nourished populations who were capable of defending the nation. Although commonly understood as a matter of domestic politics, social security was thus also about national security and ensuring the efficiency of the military machine.

NATIONAL SECURITY, THE COLD WAR, AND SECURITY STUDIES

The association of security with military security became far more explicit during and after the Second World War. The Cold War placed 'national security' centre stage and fostered the emergence of 'security studies' as an important sub-discipline of international relations (Krause and Williams 1997, McSweeney 1999). To put it simply, while social security pursues the full and fair distribution of the basic necessities of human flourishing, national security measures seek to protect the state and its territories principally by political and military means. Social security springs from a larger theory of social justice that recognizes a collective interest in securing the rights and basic needs of individual citizens. National security by contrast has its historic roots in theories of power politics that see state survival as reliant upon a willingness to take special measures to tackle threats exterior to its existence (Lustgarten and Leigh 1994: ch. 1, Neocleous 2008: ch. 3).

National security by definition conceives security principally in geographic terms, to be upheld most effectively at the borders of nation states but also by security services and armies that act beyond domestic borders in the name of the national interest. Passports, border controls, and immigration services have become crucial in making safe the boundaries of the nation state. Overt development of military defence and covert development of security and intelligence services both play key roles in the militarization of security. Hence the observation by Buzan *et al.*:

The special nature of security threats justifies the use of extra-ordinary measures to handle them. The invocation of security has been the key to legitimizing the use of force, but more generally it has opened the way for the state to mobilize, or take special powers, to handle existential threats.

(Buzan *et al.* 1998: 21)

Readings of the Cold War are complex and contested, but for present purposes can be summarized as follows. After the Second World War, the superpowers America and the Soviet Union sought to gain ascendancy by developing their military prowess and, in particular, their nuclear arms capacity, as well as by building large bloc alliances. Security was thought to lie in maintaining both conventional and nuclear capabilities superior to those held by one's rivals, such that if deterrence failed, one could reasonably expect to win a nuclear war (Freedman 2004: ch. 1). Central to this security strategy was a sophisticated political and psychological game of posturing and the seemingly inexorable expansion of nuclear arms.[4]

Given the capacity of the nuclear arms race to wreak devastation on humankind, it is perhaps unsurprising that it was accompanied by the urgent promotion of strategic security studies devoted to controlling and containing nuclear proliferation and attaining stability without resort to force. Strategic security studies are enormously complex, ranging across politics, international relations, military, and war studies (Buzan 1991, Terriff *et al.* 2005, Williams 2008). The questions addressed by security studies are similarly diverse but commonly relate to the use, or threatened use, of force and the disposition to resist or reject this. At the risk of oversimplification, these questions can be reduced to one: 'how much is enough?' In calculating the optimum level of security provision needed for deterrence, strategists faced the dilemma of how to rein in an untrammelled arms race that, despite considerable costs, would not deliver any increase in security and yet maintain a position of superiority and strategic advantage should conflict prove unavoidable (Kolodziej 2005: 90–1, Freedman 2004). The way out of this dilemma was a rational, if incongruous, commitment to cooperation through arms negotiations (the so-called Strategic Arms Limitations or 'SALT' talks), which resulted in agreements to end nuclear testing in the atmosphere; to create a hotline for use during crises; and to halt proliferation to third-party states. It also led to the development of independent forces (for example, the military wing of NATO), which sought to assert global security over the specific interests of rival superpowers.

If the Cold War was dominated by a militaristic conception of security as best secured through military deterrence and defensive measures, it also gave birth to peace and conflict resolution research that focused on international cooperation, and the development of an 'international order'. These developments can be discerned also in the emergence of peace studies and international development programmes, which posed a deliberate challenge to strategic and war studies. Conventional security studies were also increasingly contested by feminist perspectives that seek to emphasize the gender-specific nature of militaristic conceptions of security (Terriff *et al.* 2005: ch. 4).

World political events also have played a central role in shifting conceptions of security and the optimum means of its pursuit. The fall of the Berlin Wall in November 1989 and the break-up of the former Soviet Union; the emerging politics of environmental change and global warming; and larger efforts to promote security at regional, communal, and even individual levels have all contributed to successive re-conceptualizations of security. Hence the emergence of terms such as 'environmental security' and 'human security' – of which more below. The conclusion of the Cold War brought about the end of a security era that had been based on a bipolar world politics of nuclear deterrence and mutually assured destruction. However, it also gave rise to a new global order in which regional, religious, and ethnic conflicts moved centre stage. Intra-state conflict in the former Yugoslavia; genocide in Rwanda, the Sudan, and elsewhere in Africa; and the political and ethnic violence consequent on the break-up of the former Soviet Union are just some salient examples of the new threats to security. Over two million people have been killed in conflict situations over the last decade; many more have been made orphans, were maimed, abducted, abused or raped.[5] The scale of destruction wrought by these conflicts has generated a new security agenda that is only just beginning to attract criminological attention (Woolford 2006).

The collapse of superpower politics and the rise of new security hotspots in transitional states and conflict situations towards the end of the twentieth century have raised questions about the centrality of the nation state to the maintenance of security. These developments resulted in a new concern with 'human emancipation' and the security of peoples. This broadening of the security agenda subsequently promoted the development of critical security studies which seeks to challenge established security thinking and scholarship (Booth 1991, Krause and Williams 1997, Wyn-Jones 1999).

HUMAN SECURITY

As the immediacy of large-scale nuclear threat receded in the post-Cold War era, it has become possible to focus upon previously neglected issues and to recognize that economic, societal, environmental, and health problems also pose significant threats to security. In many countries, external and military threats have been overshadowed by domestic problems of poverty, starvation, disease, pollution, sectarian and ethnic violence, and human rights abuses. Security is now seen to lie in the provision of the basic necessities of human flourishing and the promotion of human rights. Born out of the convergence of research and policy making in development economics, international relations, and human rights, human security has been promoted as a new paradigm that focuses not only on state sovereignty but also the security of peoples. Human security is predicated upon the belief that the chief threats to security arise out of deprivation, frustration, and hopelessness, which breed disorder, conflict, and, in the extreme, terrorism. Whereas the traditional focus of security was upon the nation state and the protection of territory, human security makes the protection of individuals its primary referent. Its proponents see human security as a welcome conceptual breakthrough that moves beyond armed territorial security to focus on 'the security of people in their homes, jobs and communities'.[6]

The concept of human security first gained international prominence in the mid-1990s, following its adoption by the United Nations Development Programme (UNDP) as a means of advancing 'freedom from fear and want' (UNDP 1994, UN Commission on Human Security 2003). The UN contended that security would be better fostered by its integration with development, humanitarian, and human rights concerns. Security between states remains a necessary precondition but is no longer deemed sufficient to guarantee the security of people in their everyday lives. Human security is thus the motivating force behind efforts to supplement state-led protection with programmes aimed at empowering people to secure their own interests.

In policy terms, human security is addressed by political, social, environmental, economic, and cultural programmes designed collectively to furnish 'the building blocks of survival, livelihood and dignity' (UNDP 1994). Proponents of human security assert that security can be ensured only where people have a basic income, access to food, clean water, health care, minimum protection from disease (such as HIV/AIDS), and a decent environment, as well as protection from physical violence. Two important facets of human security are that the range of actors responsible for security is extended well beyond the state and that people are not simply protected but empowered to fend for themselves, not least through the development of self-governance or 'local capacity building' (Shearing and Wood 2003b: 416). Clearly human security has most resonance in the transitional and developing, as well as troubled and failing, states with which the United Nations is most engaged. The ultimate goal of human security is the promotion of human dignity and the extension of people's flourishing beyond mere survival, and in this it mirrors the social and economic rights agenda of previous decades. The state retains a vital role in developing and sustaining norms, policies, and institutions essential to protection, but this is supplemented by the expansion of human rights and the fostering of the basic goods of health, education, and employment at the micro-level (Ogata 2003).

Human security thus resists the tendency of threats like weapons of mass destruction and terrorism to solidify a narrower conception of security as state security. The conservatism and rigidity of past definitions of security in the sphere of international relations have served to exclude wider non-military issues from consideration. Instead, human security draws attention to the mundane sources of insecurity suffered by people in their everyday lives, particularly in developing countries. It also highlights the ways in which pursuit of state security can trample human rights and impede humanitarian action, not least in conflict situations, emergency conditions, and in the name of combating terrorism. Whereas traditionally security is principally defensive, human security signifies a commitment to developing and implementing creative positive solutions to sources of insecurity. From its origins within the UN and international development agencies, human security has since become an important tool for national policy makers, policy analysts, and lobbyists. By appropriating the term 'security', they convey a sense of urgency and consequence that attracts public attention and governmental resources to the otherwise low-profile field of development. As a tool of political campaigning, therefore, human security has had considerable success and has become a prominent and powerful term of art.[7]

By design, human security extends the definition of 'threat' well beyond that which has traditionally been classified as threatening state security. It is arguable that human security has deliberately been formulated without any clear definitional boundaries. Its definitional elasticity is justified on the grounds that it is 'all encompassing', 'holistic', and 'inclusive', but this has not forestalled debate about the utility of so broadly defined a concept (Paris 2001, MacFarlane and Khong 2006), what threats it should encompass, and how best it can be achieved. Proponents of an expansive concept argue that the security agenda should be widened to include hunger, disease, environmental disaster and other such threats on the grounds that these kill far more people than war, genocide, or terrorism (United Nations Development Program 1994: 23). The broadest usage of human security extends even to threats to human dignity. Proponents of this broader concept, most powerfully the UN, argue that these hazards are so interrelated, particularly in developing countries, that it cannot make sense to distinguish military threat or violence from the larger sources of insecurity. It is the very breadth of human security that is said to furnish its rhetorical force, its ability to encompass divergent interests, and to act as 'glue' holding together diverse states, development agencies, and NGOs.

Others, however, propose a narrower concept of human security, focusing upon violent threats to individuals (King and Murray 2001–2). Though they acknowledge that the expansiveness of human security has clearly served the political interest of coalition building, which explains much of its success on the international scene, this broad alliance of interests has been made possible only by the imprecision of the term. Human security is said to be 'slippery by design' (Paris 2001: 88) and its broad usage so expansive and vague as to lack analytical clarity. Such an all-encompassing concept is said to be of little use as a basis for policy analysis or academic research. Unsurprisingly, therefore, some academics have attempted to formulate a more precise definition and to develop rigorous measures by which threats to human security can be calculated and averted, particularly through risk assessment and prevention (King and Murray 2001–2). In this project lies a possible connection between human security and policing broadly conceived. For human security has a clear resonance with the historical, continental European understanding of policing as integral to ideas of good government, the condition of order in the community, and the prerequisites to good order (Kneymeyer 1980, Dubber 2005).

Whereas the security of the state was traditionally thought of as the end goal of international relations, human security suggests that it ought properly to be seen as the means to securing the protection of individuals. Understood this way, securing the civil liberties and personal safety of individuals is a major constituent of national security properly conceived (Lustgarten and Leigh 1994: 5). The interests of the state and the individual ought not be regarded as at odds, still less locked in a zero-sum game, but seen rather in a positive relationship of mutual assurance. Human security also recognizes that both objective and subjective security rely on more than political and military action against predetermined threats (be they military or criminal).

Just as international relations has arguably focused on military threats to the exclusion of domestic stability, so much contemporary crime policy has taken a militaristic form – fighting crime, the war on drugs – and paid insufficient attention to the deep structural sources of social order (Reiner 2006). Security need not only be used as a rhetorical device for shifting the debate from the causes of insecurity to the fight against it but can also be fostered by greater concern with the prerequisites of peace – for which criminologists might substitute a stable, well-ordered society.

SECURITIZATION

This brief history of the concept of security has made amply clear its power to mobilize political and economic resources. And yet this has led to a tendency to promote policies in the name of security that sacrifice competing interests and values to its more pressing claims (Loader 2002). The main problem is that security is at its most powerful when it is asserted as a basic right or fundamental good. But to do so has a tendency to foreclose debate about its priority or relationship with other goods (though see Lazarus 2007). Where security is said to be a prerequisite of, and therefore logically prior to, all other goods (aside from subsistence), then welfare, employment, health, and education necessarily take second place. The claims of security budgets prevail over other priorities and the powers demanded by the state in its name brook no challenge. The result is a depoliticization of security that is inimical to discussion about its proper place in political and social life.

Critical security scholars have warned of the ethical and political implications of viewing diverse social, economic, and political problems through the single lens of security (Waever 1995, Krause and Williams 1997, Buzan *et al.* 1998, Wyn-Jones 1999). The widening of security, such that it is 'stretched to breaking point' (Freedman 2003: 753), has adverse analytical consequences as well – too expansive a concept of security risks intellectual incoherence. If security is extended to embrace all that is necessary for human flourishing, it becomes the study of everything and nothing (Wyn-Jones 1999: 126). Viewing economic, social, health, and educational problems through the lens of security distorts our understanding of them and may dictate policies inimical to their proper solution (Wyn-Jones 1999: 107). Making social or economic policy in the name of security may be a way of enhancing its priority and attracting more resources but potentially has a distorting effect, captured by the term 'securitization'.

The securitization of political issues and public policy has a worrisome tendency to demote other concerns and to legitimize emergency powers. The danger is that competing interests, not least civil liberties, tend to be sacrificed to the more pressing claims of security. Furthermore, securitization of socio-economic problems has the effect of depoliticizing what are fundamentally political issues. For example, the creation of the European Union as an economic free trade zone has arguably been transmuted into a security engine for the protection of its members' interests. In its external relations 'fortress Europe' has been charged with developing barriers and sanctions to protect itself from a feared influx of refugees and asylum-seekers from poorer or politically unstable countries. The extent to which Europe today is being 'governed through security' is a matter of live debate. Some argue that, as a consequence, European political identity is being constructed negatively around the threats to safety posed by those outside the Union (Loader 2002), while others might consider this an unduly negative reading of the potentialities of the European Union.

Accordingly Wyn-Jones identifies as a central dilemma of international relations the question: 'should groups abandon the mobilization potential that is undoubtedly generated by using the term "security"?' (Wyn-Jones 1999: 109). It is a question equally germane to criminology. On the one hand, drawing a problem under the mantle of security gives it a special status and enhances the prospects of it receiving urgent and effective attention. On the other, this strategy simultaneously risks it being subsumed by the security agenda. The attendant danger is that securitization becomes a technique for legitimating political decisions precisely because the goal of security grants 'the state almost carte blanche powers to protect it' (Neocleous 2007a: 38). Securitizing questions that ought properly to be the subject of debate has the effect of limiting scrutiny and short-circuiting usual liberal democratic procedures for deliberation.

A parallel example can be found in the field of crime prevention. When substantial governmental funds are made available under the remit of crime prevention, local authorities quickly learn to recast housing, urban redevelopment, and youth policies as crime prevention programmes. The consequence, however, is not merely a presentational repackaging of these policies around crime prevention in order to secure funding but a fundamental shift in priorities, modes of thought, and orientation of programmes that may be only remotely connected with crime reduction. Public policy making is similarly distorted by the security agenda. One common argument is that since security already extends into social and economic policy we had better acknowledge its depth and breadth. It might be countered, however, that to securitize public policy licenses inherently defensive, non-democratic forms of decision making and the regularization of extraordinary measures. It is for these reasons, among others, that some commentators in the field of national security call for the desecuritization of policy so far as is possible (Waever 1995).

Debate continues as to whether, and to what degree,

broadening the meaning, as the notion of human security does, might overcome the defensive and combative aspects of securitization. Perhaps the application of 'security' to a widening range of policy fields will have the effect of altering its meaning. Certainly the widespread adoption of the term 'human security' has shifted conceptions of security some significant distance from the Cold War sense of responding to threats through defensive military action. This said, the traditional meaning of 'security' is not easily overborne by attaching new prefixes. 'Security', in its traditional sense, has considerable rhetorical force, and that force is a potent lever, which is one of the reasons why reference to security is so politically attractive in the first place.

In order to delve beneath the rhetoric, a profitable test is to ask whether a proposal made in the name of security addresses a real threat; whether it does so effectively; whether it is right to take the measures proposed; and whether those who resort to the rhetoric of security do so honestly or in order to achieve some other end entirely. The reality of the threat, the efficacy of the response, and the sincerity of the reference to security are empirical questions – though not always readily testable. The question of whether a measure proposed in the name of 'security' is right is, ineluctably, a normative one. By critically scrutinizing resort to the language of security, it may be possible both to contest its meaning and question its deployment (Goold and Lazarus 2007: ch. 1). Challenging the rhetorical usage of security may go some way to meeting the larger objections raised by those who condemn creeping securitization. The indelible association of security with defensive action against threat and the negative baggage surrounding the term are reasons to be wary of accepting security as a lens through which to view wider social, economic, and political problems. Criminology's own debates around moral panics, the culture of control, and penal populism provide ample evidence of the dangers that arise when crime becomes the organizing motif of public life (Cohen 1980, Garland 2001, Pratt 2007, Reiner 2007). Human security may seek to present a softer, less objectionable face to security but arguably does not entirely succeed in vanquishing these objections to the larger problem of securitization.

CONCLUSION

This brief genealogy reveals that the concept of security has a long history, during which it has moved from being an underdeveloped, imprecise idea to a subject of so much academic and political attention that it is now, if anything, an overdeveloped, though contested, concept. It also reveals that, at least from the eighteenth century, security has been a dominant component of modern governmental rationality (Burchell *et al.* 1991: 20) and a core justification of the state itself. As such, changing conceptions of security are deeply implicated in changing accounts of the state, its role and responsibilities. It is therefore hardly surprising that the dominant players in security studies have, until very recently, been in disciplines such as political science, political theory, and international relations. Criminology is a latecomer to the security field and, if it is to build upon the insights and advances in theoretical enquiry, it needs to engage more explicitly than it has done thus far with existing genres of security scholarship.

3

NEW DISTRIBUTIONS
OF SECURITY

INTRODUCTION

As we have seen, the dominant historical conception of
security has been that of national security. Security, in crude
terms, meant the defence of national borders by military,
intelligence or security services, immigration and customs
authorities. More recently it has been extended down to
encompass the security of communities and even individuals;
up to incorporate international peacekeeping, supranational
policing and security systems, international alliances, and
organizations; and horizontally to encompass political, economic, social, and environmental terrains. As Rothschild has
observed, security is

> diffused in all directions from national states, including
> upwards to international institutions, downwards to regional or
> local governments, and sideways to nongovernmental organ-
> izations, to public opinion and the press, and to abstract forces
> of nature or of the market. The geometry ... is ... of dizzying
> complexity.

(Rothschild 1995: 55)

This complexity is reduced only a little by our focus on the mapping of security as it pertains to crime, not least because patterns of distribution of security in respect of crime are themselves changing rapidly.

The pursuit of security remains synonymous with the role of the modern state and the guarantee of security is one of the most politically contested of its responsibilities (Lazarus 2007). This chapter focuses on changes in the contemporary politics and distribution of security, perhaps the most important of which are the challenges to the state dominance posed by developments above, beyond, and below government (Loader 2000: 327–8). Mapping these developments is a necessary precursor to charting and describing the new distributions of security that result. And this cartographic exercise is an essential preliminary to the normative reflections that follow on the role of the state and of non-state actors in security provision, and the defence of security as a public good. Perhaps the key fact of contemporary security politics is that the state's (in any event relatively recent and largely theoretical) monopoly of security is being dispersed among non-governmental, private, and community-based actors. This dispersal has profound implications, not least for democratic values. It has engendered a lively debate between those who hold that the defence of strong state institutions is essential for the preservation for democracy and those who propose a more de-centred agenda (Loader and Walker 2005, Shearing 2006).

As a discipline, criminology has historically held ambivalent attitudes towards the state as Janus-headed in its security function (Lustgarten and Leigh 1994: 12ff). On the one hand, the state, with its formal monopoly on force, figures in criminological literature as the principal source of public protection and shield against harm (Loader and Walker 2005). State institutions provide the main mechanisms for ensuring that rights and interests are respected, and the maintenance of a state monopoly of force limits the excesses that might result were justice left in private hands, and inhibits vigilantism and the activities of the Mafia, Yakuza, and other protection rackets (Gambetta 1993, Varese 2001, Hill 2003). If state institutions do not always abide by the letter of the law, they are nonetheless the primary means of upholding the rule of law. On the other hand, it is precisely the state's prerogative to employ force that has cast it also as a primary threat to individual liberty (Neocleous 2008: 32ff). It is against the agents of the state that the individual suspect in the interrogation room, police or prison cell must be protected. The exercise of police powers in the name of security are thus simultaneously applauded and resisted as the state stands both as provider of and, simultaneously, threat to the security of the individual. Added to which, this is a field in which political allegiances and strongly held beliefs as to the proper role of the state underpin divergent positions that are probably irreconcilable.

PUBLIC AND PRIVATE SECURITY PROVISION

Whereas once it was assumed that the welfare state was the optimal means for securing the health, happiness, and security of the population, the ascendancy of neoliberalism has challenged the key tenets of welfare economics. Neo-liberalism espouses the view that the welfare state creates a culture of dependency, inhibits risk-taking essential to the flourishing of enterprise, and is expensive and inefficient in its provision of goods (Hayek 1960). According to this position, encouraging individuals to take greater responsibility for their welfare and promoting and permitting market transactions in place of state provision is cheaper and more efficient than state provision (Ericson *et al.* 2000: 538). Yet even the most committed libertarians accept that the state should retain responsibility for the provision of basic security. This minimalist role is typically captured by the idea of the 'night-watchman state' which includes responsibility for, but does not extend much beyond, policing, judicial, penal, and military systems.

Nonetheless the effect of the free market philosophy promoted by neoliberalism has been to encourage considerable expansion of private enterprise even in respect of these core functions: hence the rise of the private security industry (of which we will say more in Chapter 5). Even in respect of security, the proposition that states govern more effectively at a distance has resulted in a withdrawal of the state from the active delivery of services ('rowing') to their direction ('steering') (Osborne and Gaebler 1992). This withdrawal from active delivery has been widely described by political scientists as connoting the rise of the regulatory state (Braithwaite 2000) or the state that 'governs at a distance'. Whether and to what extent this has effected a withdrawal by the state, even in those Western jurisdictions where it is most pronounced, is doubted by those who observe that the privatization of services and the failures of self-regulation have provoked ever greater state regulation (Moran 2003). And this is evidenced by the recent proliferation of legislation in many Western countries seeking to regulate the provision of private security services and the rise of private military companies. Friedrich identifies a 'chain of coercion' by which states routinely reassert the right to determine what poses an external or internal security threat, to specify the legitimate means to counter it, and even tightly to control the actual operation of security agents (Friedrichs 2008: 6–7). Given that moves to regulatory governance of market society were prompted by the economics of neoliberalism and Hayekian demands for a minimal state, it is particularly ironic that they appear to have resulted in more government intervention rather than less (Levi-Faur 2005: Preface 6, Crawford 2006a).

Neoliberal political analysis has tended to assume that historically the state was the central actor and law the central mechanism of regulatory governance (Hood 1998). Arguably, focus upon the state and state laws neglects forms of non-state regulation that were and remain important to the conduct of security governance. Although Scott describes non-state regulatory regimes as signifying the rise of a 'post-regulatory state' (Scott 2004), others like Braithwaite and Levi-Faur argue that regulation is not reducible to, but extends far beyond, the state. This more expansive, pluralistic interpretation of regulation is captured in such epithets as 'regulatory society' and 'regulatory capitalism' (Levi-Faur 2005, Braithwaite and Levi-Faur 2008). Much of this chapter builds on these ideas to explore the changing shape of the state and the increasingly varied and variegated means by which security is delivered.

The picture is further complicated by the fact that the changing relationship between the state and non-state actors no longer permits the drawing of a bright line between public and private (Shapland and van Outrive 1999). Relations between different ventures in security are so complex that the very distinction between public and private is increasingly blurred (Jones and Newburn 1998: ch. 8, Marx 2001), not least through strategies of responsibilization (Garland 2001: 124–7), hybridization, and mechanisms of delegation (Crawford 2003). The demarcation is also transgressed by the transfer of public services to private providers; by state regulation through the licensing, inspection, and auditing of the private security industry; and also by private sponsorship of state policing, for example, through the provision of hardware or even vehicles (in some US states the police are, quite literally, 'brought to you by Toyota'). Mapping these relations exposes deep ligatures between public and private – a phenomenon nicely captured by O'Reilly's analysis of the 'state-corporate symbiosis' (O'Reilly forthcoming) that occurs, for example, where transnational security consultancies (such as Control Risks, Diligence, Kroll, and The Risk Advisory Group) are deployed to advise 'where the interests of "high politics" and private finance intersect' (Walker 2003: 126). Political concern about the antagonistic, competitive, or simply antithetical aspects of the public/private relationship has tended to obscure the degree to which professional interaction, reciprocity, even mutual dependency, now characterize working relations between the public and private spheres in the pursuit of security (Feeley 2002, Vindevogel 2005).

THE BLURRING OF INTERNAL AND EXTERNAL SECURITY

Security conceived principally as an internal problem locates the main threat to safety as deriving from groups within the domestic polity. Risk assessment and classification of suspect groups targets those deemed to pose the greatest threat. In part-political constructions, these sub-populations vary over time. In Britain they range historically from the 'dangerous and perishing classes' of the nineteenth century through the 'welfare dependants' of the Thatcher era and the 'new age travellers' of the 1990s to the socially excluded, the anti-social, and the radicalized Muslim youth of the present day. This last example highlights the difficulty of drawing a clear line between internal and external security, not least because internal sources of perceived threat may have external roots (Bigo 2006). Part of the shock that followed the London bombings in 2005 and that has accompanied subsequent attempts is the realization that the perpetrators are 'home-grown' terrorists inspired by what was hitherto seen as the foreign ideology of Al-Qaeda.

Where security is primarily focused upon internal threats to social order, responsibility tends not only to reside with the state but is also ascribed to communities, housing associations, and even families (Garland 2001: 59). Where security is conceived primarily as a response to external threats, responsibility tends to rest more closely with the state. In Germany, for example, *Innere Sicherheit* remains tied to the activities of the state in large part because it primarily connotes threats deriving from outside the nation (Krasmann 2007). Whether from international, organized, or cross-border crimes, the German concept of *Innere Sicherheit* envisions the primary threats to security as external. Standing at the 'crossroads' of Europe between East and West, Germany's geopolitical history conceives *Innere Sicherheit* as threatened principally by *Ausländerkriminalität* – a conceptual 'hold-all' connoting crime by foreigners, as well as immigrants, asylum-seekers, and non-German nationals within Germany (Albrecht 2000), and underpinning a *Feindstrafrecht* (or enemy penology) that legitimates what Krasmann has termed a 'renaissance of sovereign power' (Krasmann 2007: 308). Yet the fact that third-generation immigrants to Germany continue to be conceived as posing an external threat points again to the difficulty of maintaining any clear distinction between external and internal security.

The terrain is complicated further by the fact that measures once thought necessary only in the high security arena of national borders and airports are now extended to the domestic hinterland. This expansion of security measures against external threats to affect the daily round of domestic policing has provoked the acute observation that 'the border is everywhere' (Feeley and Simon 1994: 181). And yet it is questionable whether borders can any longer be seen as purely geographical or even physical entities. Airports and rail termini place borders well inside national boundaries. Flows of information, money, and services are largely electronic. Virtual borders are generated by visa and passport requirements set well in advance of physical travel. Whereas globalization underwrites freedom of movement, the pursuit of security often seeks to control and limit the mobility of those deemed hostile to national security or public safety. Against the economic pull to open up borders stands the undoubted counter-pressure to resist the influx of migrants by strengthening border security.

At the international level, too, the dimensions of security are often more complex than an internal and external distinction would suggest. Membership of large supra-national security alliances such as Schengen, Europol, and NATO blurs the distinction between national interests. Across Europe the falling of borders is eroding the difference between internal and external threat, though the lowering of internal borders has been mirrored by the raising of external ones to create 'Fortress Europe' (Loader 2002). Although within Europe there are no border controls between those jurisdictions that have implemented the rules laid down under the Schengen Agreement and the European Union legally requires the free movement of EU citizens and their dependants across internal borders as an essential facet of economic union, freedom of internal movement is offset by the strengthening of external borders to limit immigration from outside. The perceived vulnerability of physical borders and other high-risk locales can be discerned in the new buzzword of border control: 'protective security' (Cabinet Office 2007: 6).

There is also an increasing trend towards securing countries well beyond their physical boundaries. In respect of the European Union, the border security agency Frontex (from the French *Frontières extérieures*) operates extensively in neighbouring countries beyond the formal boundaries of the European Union. Likewise, national governments police their borders long before would-be immigrants enter their territory. For example, UK borders and customs authorities screen passengers in French and Belgian checkpoints before they even depart for Britain, instituting what Aas deftly defines as 'security-at-a-distance' (Aas forthcoming). As immigration authorities and customs officials seek to defend national security against illegal immigrants, suspect criminals, and would-be terrorists long before they arrive at national borders, by targeting points of departure in overseas ports and airports and intercepting boats smuggling people or goods while still at sea, it is no longer clear that the security border remains at the physical boundaries of the nation state (Weber forthcoming).

Even before 9/11, the conspicuous 're-securitization' of Europe was an important theme in the creation of a common European identity. To the established 'hard security' of border controls was joined a newly emergent 'soft security' of communication technologies that now form the backbone of 'the European Information Society' (Levi and Wall 2004: 198–9). According to Levi and Wall, the new pan-European security technologies or 'mass surveillance assemblage' (Levi and Wall 2004: 205) have profound implications, in terms not only of the potential threat to individual privacy, but also the questionable accuracy of surveillance systems, and the tensions between public and private interests that result from practices like data merging and data retention (Levi and Wall 2004: 208). Not only do the new security architecture and new surveillance technologies lead to unexpected and sometimes unwarranted intrusions into our everyday lives, but they may also generate new forms of criminal activity (Wall 2007).

The new European security society has profound implications for the meaning of national identity, and poses even greater challenges for its protection (Walker 2003: 117). Loader poses the question explicitly: 'is Europe today being governed through security and, if so, with what effects? (Loader 2002: 125) His answer is that new arrangements for intergovernmental cooperation and the emergence of supranational security institutions – together with the resultant professional practices and cultures, governmental institutions and discourses, and lay mentalities – create a European identity that is constructed negatively 'in defensive opposition to an apprehended array of "existential threats" to "Europe" and its security' (Loader 2002: 145). Developing an alternative conception of a civic European identity is, for Loader, essential to the task of avoiding the costs of 'securitization' and ensuring the democratic governance of policing and security in Europe. At the same time, membership of supranational bodies, such as the European Union, has tended to license, even encourage, the aspirations of regional and ethnic groups to assert their independence, often against the perceived security interests of the nation state.

Even the distinction between national and international security can no longer be easily drawn. The international balance of power relies partly upon the hope that independent nation states pursuing their own security agendas will produce a relatively stable equilibrium, and partly on establishing a system of international security committed to shared responsibility and common action against aggressors (Freedman 2003: 755). Collective security is an important antidote to the security dilemma posed by the fact that the efforts of one state to defend its own security may pose, or be deemed to pose, a source of insecurity to other states. Since no single supranational body can provide security, international security is perhaps better thought of as a system reliant on dialogue, open channels of communication, summit meetings, agreements and accords. All this explains the continued commitment to the Strategic Arms Limitations (SALT) talks even, or perhaps especially, at the height of the Cold War discussed in the last chapter.

Nowhere is the tension between enhancing security and defensive or exclusionary policies more clearly illustrated than in the contemporary politics of immigration (Dauvergne 2007: 544–5). Finding the optimal relationship between security and the free flow of people and goods is the big dilemma of modern states and the pressure upon governments to resolve the tension between them is acute. Transnational organized crime, trafficking, and terrorism are core sources of contemporary insecurity whose scale and potential costs are unprecedented. Historically high levels of migration have caused governments to identify immigration as a potential threat to national identity and state security (though it is arguable that this conceals deeper concerns about limiting foreign access to scarce internal resources, social service provision, and maintaining control over labour markets).[1] While classical conceptions of security focused on defending the sovereignty and territorial integrity of the nation state, it is doubtful whether nations' efforts to enhance national identity and national security through exclusionary immigration policies any longer make sense (Dauvergne 2007: 545).

The global nature of contemporary security threats means that the defence of national sovereignty loses its *raison d'être*. In the modern global order, security is served as much by ensuring economic prosperity as by conventional defensive measures. The conceptual expansion of national security to include 'economic well-being' has given the state a new interest in securing economic stability abroad. Managing migration remains a core element in contemporary security politics but the exclusionary impulses of defending national identity and guarding against military and terrorist threats are counterbalanced by economic interests. The pursuit of material economic power now lies high on the security agenda (Rudolph 2003). Against the political impulse to exclusion runs a powerful counter-economic impulse therefore to openness. As critical security scholars and advocates of human security have made clear, economic security is an essential first step towards global security. Yet at the same time the link made between national and economic security has also been used to justify the introduction of repressive security and surveillance measures, border controls, and other defensive immigration policies (Bosworth 2008) which are as much about defending as about opening up markets.

CHANGING SECURITY DISTRIBUTION

The already faltering public/private dichotomy and internal/external security divide are now further eroded by the rapid development of the private security industry and the proliferation of security providers that together transform the map of security provision. Much academic energy has gone into charting these shifts in the distribution of security. The complex new arrangements have variously being described as the 'pluralization' of provision (Johnston 2003, Dupont and Wood 2006: 3); the 'multilateralization' of security (Johnston 2006: 33); and the 'mixed economy' of security provision (Crawford *et al.* 2005). Dorn and Levi observe that the increasing role of the private security industry in assisting and acting as a substitute for the public sphere leads to 'greater permeability' of the borders between private and public security (Dorn and Levi 2007). Though all these scholars plot patterns of security distribution differently, their common consensus is that traditional maps will not help us.

Security distribution has historically been described principally by reference to those who provide it – hence talk of the 'extended policing family' (Johnston 2003), of 'light blue policing', and of 'grey' areas of intermixed public/private provision (Hoogenboom 1991). When public bodies hire private corporations to provide security services for public buildings and public space or, alternatively, when public police sell their services to corporations (the subcontracting of public policing services to football stadia is a case in point) it is not clear whether the resulting provision is public or private. A private security firm may be paid for a public body to patrol a public institution but it is questionable whether this constitutes the fulfilment of a public function or a more amorphous new genre of security provision. Together these changes result in a larger shift from the 'solid state technology' of formal criminal justice systems to the altogether more fluid, impermanent set of relations that occur under 'liquid security' (Zedner 2006a). Other observers see security itself as forming tangible new formations variously described by a series of graphic metaphors that include security 'patchworks', 'quilts', 'bubbles', 'corridors', 'mosaics', 'webs', 'networks', and 'nodes'.

The notion of security quilt captures the patchwork quality of provision (Ericson 1994, Wakefield 2003: ch. 3) in which providers take responsibility for different substantive or geographical areas of security but whose whole is made up of tightly sewn, interdependent pieces forming, if not a coherent entity, at least something approaching blanket coverage. This comforting imagery is challenged by those who see security coverage as being altogether more 'frayed' and 'fragmented' (Crawford and Lister 2004: 427). So, for example, Rikagos and Greener identify security as residing only in 'bubbles of governance' that encircle those within them, leaving those outside to inhabit increasingly precarious unprotected realms (Rigakos and Greener 2000).[2] Similarly, Sheptycki identifies 'corridors of security' (most obviously airports and airlines) through which a mobile class of professionals moves in the global free market economy (Sheptycki 2002: 144). The centrality of the state is further challenged by the growing market in security products and services (of which more in Chapter 5) which creates a mosaic of private 'contractual communities' such as gated residential areas, shopping malls, university campuses, sports and leisure facilities, as well as the virtual communities of credit and insurance. Together, this expanding archipelago of private security provision creates what Shearing terms 'an emerging "neo-feudalism" ' (Shearing 2001b: 211), which results in palpable tensions between the justice-orientation of the state police and the risk-orientation of private security providers.

Others place less emphasis on the spatial distribution of security provision than the linkages that form and multiply among providers. Network analysis has been particularly important in seeking to establish the relations and links among different security agents that together make up a web-like structure of security provision (Crawford and Lister 2004). It is a matter of continuing debate whether the resultant relationships between security providers can reasonably be described as cohesive networks. Some, like Dupont, consider the concept of the network to be a powerful one, able not only to describe the heterogeneity of actors involved and the physical relations of distribution but also to explore the dynamics of security relations that transcend borders, time, and space; the adaptive strategies of public and private institutions; and their ability to mobilize economic, political, cultural, and social 'capital' through security networks (Dupont 2004, 2006). Others, like Crawford, are more sceptical of the importance of networks. Crawford argues that in 'studying networked governance for its own sake and in its own terms of reference, we can come to miss the manner in which networks supplement (and supplant) the formal authority of government . . . the empirical evidence from the UK at least is that co-ordinated security networks are the exception rather than the norm' (Crawford 2006a: 460, Jones and Newburn 2002). The metaphor of the network thus arguably presents an overly organized image of what are altogether more fragmentary and disconnected arrangements.

Arising out of network analysis is a newer focus upon 'nodes' that shifts focus from the lines of interaction to the points of intersection at which security is actually delivered. Nodal analysis as a descriptive and explanatory tool has attracted an enthusiastic following among a group of security scholars led by Clifford Shearing (Shearing 2001a, Shearing and Wood 2003b, Johnston 2006, Wood and Shearing 2007). But as Wood's analysis makes clear, there are also normative consequences to its adoption: 'Put simply, the nodal view assumes that governance is never fully actualized by a single node, even though some nodes may indeed be hegemonic' (Wood 2006: 219). By implication state scepticism creeps back in the guise of an expository device that regards all nodes as legitimate sources of security. Yet, as Crawford makes clear, the 'residualization' of the state implicit in the privileging of multiple security suppliers and the consequent development of security as a club good available only to those with access cannot help but have adverse consequences for policing as a public good, not least insofar as it results in discrimination, segregation, and exclusion (Crawford 2006b). To the claims and criticisms of 'nodal governance' as a means of governing security we will return in Chapter 7.

THE POLITICAL ECONOMY OF SECURITY

These differing conceptions of security are often presented as principally descriptive or analytical but it should by now be clear that they rest on divergent conceptions of the role of the state. Although differential security provision is clearly not predetermined by the political economy of any given nation state, it would appear nonetheless to be closely influenced by prevailing political ideas (Cavadino and Dignan 2006, Tonry 2007). Rose argues that despite the seeming incoherence and heterogeneity of contemporary security strategies: '[t]hey can be broadly divided into two families: those that seek to regulate conduct by enmeshing individuals within circuits of inclusion and those that seek to act upon pathologies through managing a different set of circuits, circuits of exclusion' (Rose 2000: 187). At the risk of over-generalization: individualist neoliberal societies like the United States tend to place the burden on private citizens to act prudentially by protecting themselves, their families, and their property (O'Malley 2001). Greater emphasis is placed on private security solutions; personal insurance; purchase of security hardware (such as burglar alarms) and personal security services; and residence within privately secured zones. At the same time, state security policies tend to focus upon identifying, isolating, and containing those thought most to threaten respectable citizens (Simon 1999). It is not surprising therefore that, in general, neoliberal countries have markedly higher rates of imprisonments than elsewhere (Whitman 2003, Lacey 2008).

More solidaristic, social democratic societies (such as Sweden and Finland) tend to maintain state, or at least collective, responsibility for security, concentrate upon safety in public rather than private or semi-private space; and focus on the fostering of social inclusion, trust, and communal safety rather than relying upon privately purchased hardware and security guards (Zedner 2003a: 175). The distinctions drawn here are crude and it is unlikely that either the individualistic or the solidaristic model will map unproblematically upon any single society, not least because societies may be more solidaristic in some aspects than others (Lacey 2008: ch. 2). To take one example, the solidarism of the German Christian-Democratic tradition is manifest in a society where (in sharp contrast to, say, America) small children walk unaccompanied to school watched over by the collective eye of the community. On the other hand this solidarism does not extend equally to guest workers, asylum-seekers, and members of immigrant communities, who are likely rather to be the subject of suspicion and blame (Albrecht 1997).

Recognizing that security is inextricably linked with the prevailing political culture is an important first step to understanding differences in its distribution and a key to comparative analysis (Cavadino and Dignan 2006). It is also a necessary preliminary to any normative debate about its just distribution and equitable provision. It should be clear by now that the increasingly spatialized nature of security creates different geographical domains with differing genres of security provision. At the same time transformations in the international political economy are further shifting relations between public and private actors, not least between states and powerful private corporations that seek to cash in on threat and disaster (Klein 2007). Whether and to what extent changes in the delivery of security affect its provision as public good, club good, or tradable commodity is a question to which we will return in Chapter 7. Suffice it to say here that explanatory accounts are inseparable from normative analysis of the rightful provenance and just distribution of security (Hope 2000, Loader and Walker 2001, Newburn 2001, Hudson 2003, Shearing and Johnston 2005, Loader and Walker 2007).

CONCLUSION

The shifting patterns of security provision described in this chapter have profound implications for the role of the state. In the larger literature of political science one can observe a growing tendency to conflate empirical observation with normative theorizing so that, instead of maintaining a critical stance towards changes in the practice and distribution of power, political scientists tend to propose new forms of governance consistent with those changes. At one level this is a pragmatic accommodation to radical changes in the delivery of public services but at another it suggests too quiescent a response to substantial erosions in the power of the state. And yet, as this chapter has revealed, the changes occurring are more varied and more complex than the 'from rowing to steering' or 'from government to governance' stories suggest, particularly if one takes account of the rather different narratives being played out in some continental European countries. The role of the state in furnishing the legal framework, and regulatory and accountability mechanisms that govern the pursuit of security, remains central to the preservation of security as a public good.

4

SECURITY, CRIME, AND CRIMINAL JUSTICE

So far we have addressed security as a concept largely independent of criminal justice, yet for criminologists the relationship between security and criminal justice is pivotal. This chapter re-examines some basic presumptions about crime and the values of criminal justice in order better to assess to what degree they are challenged by the pursuit of security; how criminal justice is being influenced and modified; and to what extent sidelined by new security practices that operate on the margins of or outside the ordinary criminal justice process. There are excellent sociologies of the changing culture, emergent *idées fixes*, technologies, and targets of contemporary crime control.[1] Criminologists have devoted themselves to identifying, delineating, and analysing these changes. Less attention has been paid to the ethical and political issues they throw up, and still less to how far existing criminal justice structures, values, and principles still apply. How, for example, does due process help the youth arbitrarily excluded from mass private property by a private security guard on grounds of appearance alone? Or, more seriously still, how does due process apply to the sexual offender whose name is placed upon a publicly available register or whose home location is publicized on the web? And what relevance do established criminal justice principles have for those subject to civil preventive orders, preventive detention, or emergency powers introduced during periods of apparent crisis? The pursuit of security places all these people outside the ordinary protections of the criminal justice system and a new normative framework for governing security is needed if their rights are to be protected.

CRIME IN THE SECURITY SOCIETY

Making sense of the impact of the pursuit of security on criminal justice requires that we first understand the fundamental changes wrought in the perception and analysis of crime. Conventionally crime has been regarded principally as a moral wrong, as social deviance, or as harm attributable to responsible individuals who can justly be held to account for their actions or omissions and subjected to penal measures designed to inculcate law-abiding behaviour (Tadros 2007a). In a radical departure from this position, neoliberal society has come to accept the normality of crime: hence Felson's well-known characterization of crime as a 'fact of everyday life' (Felson 2002) and Garland's account of crime as a 'normal social commonplace aspect of modern society' (Garland 2001: 128). In the security society, sociological explanations of crime as deviant or pathological or as the product of social deprivation, inequality, and inadequate social control give way to characterizations of crime as 'routine activity' or the exploitation of 'opportunity' by rational, calculating offenders (Felson and Clarke 1998). In part this re-conceptualization of crime derives from the declining currency of the deviancy model and concomitant loss of faith in rehabilitation (Martinson 1974, Garland 2001: ch. 3). In part it stems from the recognition that most crimes are minor property or minor public order offences and that violent and sexual offences make up a very small proportion of recorded crimes. And in part it originates in the growing influence of economic analysis of crime (Zedner 2006c).

In a striking development, in the security society, crime is seen less as a moral wrong, a threat to shared values, or a culpable act in need of punishment than as a bundle of physical, psychological, and material losses or as a potential hazard whose cost can be calculated, minimized, and insured against (Williams 2005a). Gone is the understanding of deviance as inseparable from the wider sources of misery in modern society. Crime is no longer ineradicably linked with the big social and economic problems of poverty, inequality, poor education, housing, and health care. Personal life histories, the influence of family, social class, race, gender, and economic deprivation are excluded from consideration. Characteristic is Felson's claim that 'it is a mistake to assume that crime is part of a larger set of social evils, such as unemployment, poverty, social injustice, or human suffering' (Felson 2002: 12). Instead, crime is said to result more from the multiplication of opportunity than changes in demography, social structure, or socialization processes. Wide availability of small, light, portable and high-value consumer goods (like mobile phones), mass car ownership, and increased leisure activity (in particular, the night-time economy of clubs and bars) create new temptations and new opportunities for crime as well as increased occasions for drunkenness, disorder, and interpersonal violence (Hobbs *et al.* 2003, Hadfield 2006). These opportunities are said to be more important in explaining crime rates than moral or social breakdown. Opportunity theory is heavily influenced by environmental criminology, routine activity theory, and crime pattern theory (Felson and Clarke 1998: 4). Most influential of all is rational choice theory, an offshoot of economic analysis that extends the ' "economic approach" to other areas of social life' (Hindess 1993: 542). By sharp contrast to the sociology of deviance, economic analysis assumes rational actors who make reasoned decisions within the parameters of choices available to them and within the constraints of their world-view.

A notable feature of decision making according to rational choice theory is its lack of normativity. Hence obedience to the law is explained not by reference to norms or individual reflection upon norms but according to opportunity costs. Explanations of criminality likewise proceed without reference to norms. Offenders are deemed to be rational utility maximizers and as such 'are primarily not regarded as deviant individuals with atypical motivations, but rather as simple, normal persons like the rest of us' (Eide 2000: 345). This thinking is consistent with the assumption of rational choice theory that all people have similar hierarchies of ordered preferences. Thus it is assumed not only that non-violent offending is commonplace but that it will be committed by most people where the opportunity costs are sufficiently low. Recidivism results not from a lack of moral compass or self-control but is to be expected where preferences remain stable and there is no change in the offender's perception of opportunity costs. It follows that it is possible to manipulate preferences by changing opportunity structures. The greater the perceived opportunities for low-risk gain, the more valuable and readily obtainable the goods, and the less protection surrounding them, the more attractive is criminality. Equally, closing down opportunities, ratcheting up the perceived likelihood of being caught, or the costs thereof will weigh negatively in the rational actor's calculations to inhibit offending.

For the risk-averse offender, greater certainty of detection or severity of punishment will tend to deter. Recognition that for some types of offender and indeed some types of offence (joy-riding would be a good example) the thrill of risk taking is part of the pleasure requires modification of the model. The fact that young offenders, in particular, are radically present-orientated; that they may be neither amenable to future rewards nor strongly deterred by any but the most immediate threats; that many lack self-control, are reckless and risk-loving not risk-averse; and that supposed deterrents may have currency as badges of honour in their circles (the Anti-Social Behaviour Order, or ASBO, is one such example in Britain) can all be fed into economic models without difficulty. Particularly germane is the concept of 'hyperbolic discounting', or tendency of offenders radically to discount temporally distant costs, burdens, or benefits in favour of immediate gains. Yet even acknowledging that individual attitudes towards risk vary and that risk lovers will be less susceptible to increases in certainty of detection or severity of punishment, economic analysis assumes that, overall, increasing the marginal costs of criminality results in fewer crimes.

All this has significant implications for security. Economic analysis places in doubt the traditional apparatus of the criminal justice system. Since post-hoc policing, investigation of crime, and trial are geared to the establishment of criminal liability and the ascription of guilt after the event, they contribute little to averting harms and minimizing losses before they occur. Retributive punishment requires censure and sanction of wrongful acts done. Consequentialist measures such as rehabilitation presume a deviant individual whose soul can be the subject of effective intervention. Economic analysis, on the other hand, conceives of crimes as risks to security rather than as moral wrongs and demands intervention before crimes occur, on the grounds that where the risks can be calculated it is more cost effective to prevent loss than to punish retrospectively. It also switches intervention from the soul of the perpetrator to the structural conditions of offending by targeting the opportunity rather than the offender (Felson and Clarke 1998).

This reconceptualization of crime as security risk is most

plausible in respect of property offences, low-level threats to public order, and anti-social behaviour. It is more problematic to reconstruct offences of sexual and physical violence as calculable costs. Their perpetrators continue to invite public outrage, to stand firmly within the orbit of moral censure, and to resist redefinition as mere subjects of rational calculation. Likewise those whose capacity for rational calculation is diminished by drug abuse, alcoholism, or severe personality disorders tend to be demonized as distinct dangerous classes who can be best dealt with by incarceration in the mass penal warehouses that are the hallmark of late modern penality (Simon 1999). But the important point is that the resultant rise in the prison population is less a consequence of punitivism than the pursuit of security. As Sparks observes, mass incarceration is best understood as:

> not so much an intensification of 'punitiveness' *tout court* as an increasing preoccupation with confinement as such . . . its conditions and the perfection of its security.
>
> (Sparks 2000: 136)

THE PRE-CRIME LOGIC OF SECURITY

No wonder then that security has become an important plank of domestic crime control and policing. It is articulated as a growing concern with individual and communal safety, a function of personal and community crime prevention, and manifests itself in the growing armoury of security and surveillance technologies (of which CCTV, though far from being the silver bullet it is said to be, is probably the most prominent) (Marx 1995). It has also generated a new vocabulary of risk, actuarial justice, precaution, prudentialism, moral hazard, and insurance: all formerly outside the criminological lexicon but now firmly established as criminological terms of art (O'Malley 2004a). Use of these terms is not mere sociological rhetoric – it is mirrored by substantive changes within the criminal justice system. Surveillance, situational crime prevention, and community safety initiatives, risk assessment, actuarial profiling, offender registers, and preventive orders are all now staples of criminal justice practice (Goold 2004, Zedner 2006b, 2008b). Yet the fact that these new practices are carried out by traditional criminal justice officials should not obscure the fact that they connote a significant change in the ways in which those same officials operate and in the overarching rationale within which their decision making now occurs.

The criminal justice process, the trial, and punishment practices rely upon entrenched assumptions, conventions, and principles that are thrown into question by the security society. Although crime prevention has long had a role and although inchoate offences like attempts, conspiracy, and incitement are established (though problematic) instances of criminal liability for wrongs yet to occur, the dominant logic of criminalization and punishment is retrospective. Criminal responsibility is the calling to account of those who have done wrong (Tadros 2007a) and punishment is above all an act of censure and sanction for that wrongdoing (von Hirsch 1993). By contrast the dominant logic underpinning security is pre-emptive. The post-crime logic of criminal justice is increasingly overshadowed by the pre-crime logic of security, as I have observed elsewhere:

> Security is less about reacting to, controlling or prosecuting crime than addressing the conditions precedent to it. The logic of security dictates earlier and earlier interventions to reduce opportunity, to target harden and to increase surveillance even before the commission of crime is a distant prospect.
>
> (Zedner 2007a: 265)

Conventional reliance on reactive post-hoc measures is being overlaid by a trend towards new preventive measures that seek to anticipate and forestall harms long before they occur and to maximize security proactively. Security provides a warrant for intervention and curtailment of individual liberties at earlier points in time and against as yet unspecified or remote threats. No longer must an act be 'more than merely preparatory' to trigger the criminal law of attempt. For example, in Britain under the Terrorism Act 2006, 'acts preparatory to' terrorism become an offence in their own right for the first time. Of America, Janus describes this as a move to 'radical prevention':

> radical prevention seeks to intervene where there is some sort of 'propensity' or risk of future harm, whereas routine prevention responds to actual or attempted harm. Second, radical prevention operates by substantially curtailing people's liberty before harm results, whereas in routine prevention individuals suffer deprivations of liberty only after actual harm is done or attempted.[2]

In what follows we will examine some of the more prominent changes that security has wrought in the shape, form, and orientation of criminal justice.

SURVEILLANCE

Surveillance has become a key plank of criminal justice policy fed by the development of new technologies developed first to collect data on those deemed to be members of suspect populations and, increasingly, to collect and store data on entire populations (Lyon 2007b, Goold 2009). New surveillance technologies subject more people, citizens and non-citizens, to practices of social sorting by which it is determined that some become objects of categorical suspicion to be monitored more intensively. In part the rise of surveillance is the product of technological possibility. In part it is the product of falling costs: although CCTV cameras have been around for decades, it is only in the last twenty years or so that they have become cheap enough for widespread use. Visual surveillance occurs through CCTV and satellite tracking; 'dataveillance' through data mining, collation and storage of communication records and the actual content of communications by computer software; biometrics through fingerprints, iris scans, and DNA profiling. These are just some of the key examples of new technologies that have replaced older informal social controls (Aas 2004) or have greatly increased the effectiveness of traditional bureaucratic methods of control. In part surveillance can be seen as the outcome of managerialist practices that seek economic, efficient, and effective means to screen, check, classify, and record the characteristics, communications, movements, and other activities of those who are the subject of security. And in part surveillance must be understood as a product both of the rational bureaucratic practices of modernity and insurance logics that locate security in the development of intelligence-gathering, identification, and tracking techniques (Lyon 2007a). Yet because everything can be monitored and recorded at little cost, it is no longer necessary to make resource-led choices about what or who to look at. Mass surveillance is attractive as a tool of security because it dispenses with the need to set priorities in advance.

The influence of particularly high-profile threats to security such as international and organized crime, fraud, and terrorism provide the justification for surveillance measures whose infringement of civil liberties might otherwise be deemed untenable. The 'surveillance society' has thus become the technological double of the security society, a subject of a burgeoning literature in surveillance studies (Lyon 2007b), and a source of ongoing change in policing and criminal justice practice. It has also generated a new security architecture which designs surveillance technologies and techniques into our physical and virtual surrounds, and embeds surveillance practices into everyday life (Jones 2005: 487–90). Debates about the import of surveillance technologies and their security effects have been polarized between those who see them as providing the means to more efficient policing and greater public protection and those who see them as 'heralding the advent of a dystopian and totalitarian surveillance society' (Aas *et al.* 2008: Introduction). Lying between these is a middle ground that sees surveillance as tantamount to a 'fifth utility', as part of the larger public infrastructure and less about high-level security than serving public safety in a more mundane sense.

SITUATIONAL CRIME PREVENTION

Nowhere is the use of surveillance more prominent than in the drive to prevent crime. Traditionally crime prevention has been directed at identifying and addressing the deeper roots of crime and the social and economic causes of offending. Crime prevention in the security society is less concerned with deep roots than the immediate conditions or situational aspects under which offences occur. It is the product of a neoliberal polity in which concern for collective, social, and structural dimensions is displaced by a focus on the governance of risky individuals and risky situations (Rose 1996, Reiner 2006). Social and moral considerations are dislodged by an economic rationality that is concerned less with the constitutive mechanisms of civil society than with the narrower goal of loss management. The focus thus shifts away from the retrospective workings of the criminal process, trial, and punishment, and towards the physical environments and opportunity structures in which crime is committed. The criminal justice process becomes but one tool in an array of preventive activities undertaken by the community, local authorities, and private enterprise. State policing remains important but, in significant respects, it too is moving outside the norms and conventions of the criminal justice process. Whereas crime prevention was once marginal to the working of the criminal justice state, the new prospective orientations render prevention central. Responding to crime as a moral wrong becomes secondary to estimating, averting, and minimizing losses and insuring against harm (O'Malley 1992, 2004a).

Informed by a so-called 'routine activity approach', situational crime prevention identifies three minimal preconditions of crime: 'a likely offender, a suitable target, and the absence of a capable guardian'; this trio is said to have greater predictive and explanatory capacity than any 'speculation about the source of the offender's motivation' (Clarke 1995: 100). The opportunity structure of an offence is thus not a simple physical entity but the complex interplay between potential offenders, victims, and targets. Situational crime prevention offers the possibility of making multiple small-scale, cost-efficient, and apparently effective changes. These changes include target hardening, access control, deflecting offenders, entry- and exit-screening, formal and informal (or 'natural') surveillance, target removal, and property marking, 'opportunity reduction', and 'situational controls' (Felson and Clarke 1998, Zedner 2006c). Situational crime prevention has become a key plank in governmental crime prevention policies. It also lies behind attempts to encourage potential crime victims to limit their exposure to risk and to increase levels of self-protection by altering their movements; by thinking and acting prudentially; and by buying security devices and services. This responsibilization of victims is controversial, not least because it tends towards victim-blaming and inequalities in levels of protection, and thus undermines social trust (Kleinig 2000).

RISK ASSESSMENT AND MANAGEMENT

Another important area of pre-emptive security endeavour is the domain of risk assessment and what has come to be known as the 'new penology' or 'actuarial justice' (Feeley and Simon 1992, 1994, Feeley 2004). Actuarial justice provides the underlying rationale for identifying, classifying, and managing suspect populations according to the level of risk they are perceived to pose and in advance of any wrongdoing. Risk assessment is now advanced as a central tool in the management of crime and terrorism (Ericson and Haggerty 1997, Aradau and van Munster 2007, Mythen and Walklate 2008). It is debatable whether it is driven principally by the demand for security or rather by the very possibility of calculation. Too little attention has been paid to the degree to which the growing sophistication of actuarial tools and huge advances in computational power both enable and legitimate pre-emptive intervention. Central to the growing dominance of actuarialism is its claim to furnish more reliable data about the likelihood of future offending than the subjective judgement of professionals previously relied upon. Reliance on risk assessment presumes that threats are calculable, that risky populations are identifiable impartially, according to objective criteria, and based upon reliable data (Zedner 2006b: 426, 2008b).

Yet, despite its claim to objectivity, it is questionable how far risk assessment can justifiably be considered an apolitical and objectively scientific exercise. It is far from clear that actuarial tools yield substantively different categorizations from those previously made by psychiatric experts. The indicia of risk which form the basis for actuarial modelling are no more than the product of cumulative individual human judgements (O'Malley 1992). Moreover, the very definition of risks is politicized and heavily context-dependent, while offender profiles are based as much on institutionally and socio-politically determined categories as upon scientific assessment of who poses most risk. Important here is the influence of feminist criminology and the rise of victimology in generating concern not only for victims but for *potential* victims: the development of risk-management techniques for domestic violence is a case in point (Hoyle 2008). Risk management is a policy exercise and entails distinct policy choices which have profound consequences for those directly affected (Harcourt 2007: ch. 6). Furthermore, the interplay between the evaluative process of assessing threats and the policy process of determining appropriate responses undermines any bright line between risk assessment and its management. Where the 'data' (for example, on the risk posed by sex offenders (Hood *et al.* 2002)) are less than scientific and the statistics in question a matter of political construction, risk assessment cannot safely be distinguished from the inherently political question of its management.

It follows that there is a need for a larger debate about the role and deployment of actuarial tools in the pursuit of security. The very label 'actuarial justice', although used critically by its originators, Feeley and Simon (Feeley and Simon 1994), nonetheless speaks not only of technological innovation but of a new conception of justice. The substantive consequences of actuarialism have been much explored in the wake of Feeley and Simon's seminal writing. Yet, with a few notable exceptions (Hudson 2003, Shearing and Johnston 2005), the normative ramifications of actuarialism for existing conceptions of criminal justice have been subject to little scrutiny. Yet the implications are grave, as Harcourt observes:

> the use of predictive methods has begun to distort our carceral imagination, to mold our notions of justice, without our full

acquiescence, without deliberation, almost subconsciously or
subliminally. Today we have an intuitive but deep sense that it
is just to determine punishment largely on the basis of an
actuarial risk assessment.

(Harcourt 2007: 31)

This silent incursion of actuarial thinking is all the more
surprising if one recalls the sophistication and intensity of
earlier debates over the practicality and ethics of seeking
to identify and confine dangerous offenders (Floud and
Young 1981, Radzinowicz and Hood 1981, Bottoms and
Brownsword 1982). By contrast and with remarkably little
controversy, actuarialism has challenged the dominance of
desert as the central rationale in penal theory and insinuated
itself into criminal justice decision making with the result
that risk-based sentencing is now a central feature of many
penal systems.

Why has this occurred? First, the growing dominance
of actuarialism over proportionate punishment may be
seen as symptomatic of a larger shift in political allegiance
from retributive justice to a consequentialist, security-
oriented focus on deterrence and incapacitation (Steiker
2002). Secondly, the demand to avert risk stems from
the growth of penal populism with its attendant calls for
public protection, bolstered by media-fed perceptions of
the risks of sexual predation, violent crime, and terrorist
threat (Pratt 2007: ch. 4). These political imperatives side-
line the role of criminal justice experts in favour of a quick-
fix political response to media-generated scares (Loader
2006). Together they contribute to a growing sense that
'presumption of innocence', 'proof beyond reasonable
doubt', and the requirement of proportionality in punishment are legal luxuries ill-suited to present perils (Ignatieff
2004, but see Ashworth 2006). Finally, averting disaster has
become a political imperative for governments anxious to

safeguard their reputation against the adverse fallout that inevitably occurs if harms eventuate. As the role of the state retrenches in many Western neoliberal polities, security has become a last bastion of legitimate state activity (Nozick 1974). There is consequently much more at stake in the prospect of failure in this limited domain of the state as night-watchman. Together these factors feed recourse to surveillance, crime prevention, and actuarial justice, and provide their justifying rationale and the political environment in which they flourish. As a consequence profiling software and risk-assessment tools furnish the basis for many security-based initiatives including preventive detention, indefinite detention of high-risk offenders, as well as risk management in policing, imprisonment and parole decisions that combine to alter and distort the shape of criminal justice.

CIVIL PREVENTIVE MEASURES

Important changes are occurring too in the ways that people who are deemed to pose a threat to security or public safety are dealt with. Note that it has become necessary to talk of those 'deemed to pose a threat' because the old language of suspects and offenders no longer fits the conceptual categories in play. New procedural channels and measures are being developed at the margins of the criminal justice system that seek to pre-empt future risks and operate in respect of remote harms. Many do not operate squarely within the domain of the criminal law, as once they would have done. They circumvent the protections of the criminal process by operating in parallel systems of questionable justice: according to the less exacting requirements of the civil process or enforced via hybrid systems in which breach of civil orders result in criminal sanctions (Simester and von Hirsch 2006, Zedner 2007c).

Prominent examples from Britain include, at the bottom of the scale, a growing raft of civil preventive restrictions: disqualification from driving, disqualification from acting as a company director, disqualification from working with children, travel restriction orders, and exclusion from licensed premises orders (Ashworth and Zedner 2008). Further up tariff, the Sexual Offences Prevention Order and Risk of Sexual Harm Order (RSHO), both created under the Sexual Offences Act 2003, are controversial civil preventive orders aimed specifically at protecting the public from serious sexual harm (Shute 2004: 425). In between, lie such measures as the notorious Anti-Social Behaviour Order (ASBO), first introduced under the Crime and Disorder Act 1998. The ASBO is a civil order designed to tackle behaviour that causes offence or harassment or intimidates others (Ashworth 2004, Ramsay 2004, Burney 2005) but need not be criminal. These orders require no conviction; impose wide-ranging constraints for a minimum of two years; and, if breached, may result in imprisonment for up to five years. Recent additions to this list are the Control Order against terrorist suspects (on which see Chapter 6 below) and the Serious Crime Prevention Order (SCPO) introduced under the Serious Organised Crime Act 2007. Both are hybrid civil-criminal orders that impose considerable restrictions set under a civil order made in civil proceedings, breach of which constitutes a criminal offence with a penalty of up to five years' imprisonment (Simester and von Hirsch 2006). The development of these preventive civil measures is by no means confined to Britain. Parallels can be drawn with developments elsewhere, not least the introduction of Control Orders (modelled closely on the British example) in Australia and the deployment of civil containment against sexual offenders in the US – a development that has spawned a large and critical law review literature of its own.[3]

Together these various measures can be seen as contributing to a larger security architecture erected in civil channels which sidesteps ordinary criminal process (Günther 2005: 380) and evades its strictures and protections. The labelling of these measures as preventive rather than punitive legitimates the imposition of restrictions based upon determinations of future conduct rather than attribution of blame for past action. So it is that John Monahan, a leading US proponent of risk-based sentencing, can argue: 'any risk factor that validly forecasts violence – with the exception of race or ethnicity – is a legitimate candidate for inclusion' (Monahan 2006: 395). Yet the labelling of a measure as preventive and the resort to civil measures cannot conceal the punitive burdens nonetheless imposed (Zedner 2007b). As civil measures encroach ever more on the territory of the criminal law, the safeguards of criminal proceedings, the principles of fair warning, proportionality, and certainty are overridden. Although these measures substantially extend the scope of state power to act in the name of security, they can be seen to threaten security in its older liberal conception as the security of the individual against an overbearing state. It is in recognition of this danger that Nickel rightly insists 'due process rights are security rights' (Nickel 2007).

PRECAUTION

While preventive measures have become central means of managing threats to security by those deemed to pose the highest risk, it is arguable they are being surpassed by a more recent trend towards precaution. A central tenet of contemporary public policy making is the precautionary principle that addresses the duty on public actors to avert serious or irreversible damage (Gardiner 2006). It states that in the face of serious or irreversible harm, lack of full scientific certainty shall not be used as a reason for inaction or postponement of cost-effective measures to prevent such harms (Fisher 2005: 118). In practice the logic of precaution becomes a ground not merely for action but for robust pre-emptive measures and the enactment of emergency powers in the face of the unknown (McCulloch and Carlton 2006). Whereas agents of criminal justice are required to satisfy tests as to the sufficiency of evidence before they seek to prosecute, precaution, in effect, licenses action even when evidence is not available or, if available, where it cannot or will not be disclosed. Although in origin the precautionary principle is applicable in law only in respect of grave and irreversible harms, the logic of precaution is spreading downward to provide a warrant for decision making in situations of uncertainty even where the anticipated harms are of a lesser gravity. It has come to inform an altogether less principled precautionary approach that serves as a licence for policies formulated to deal with incalculable but threatening futures.

Precaution does not require that it is possible to calculate future risks before action is taken (Haggerty 2003). Rather than relying on the identification of risky individuals, the precautionary approach treats all as possible sources of suspicion or threat. So that whereas risk-thinking stimulated the development of profiling, targeted surveillance, categorization of suspect populations, and other actuarial techniques for managing risky populations, precaution promotes pre-emptive action to avert potentially grave harms using undifferentiated measures that target everyone. Whereas risk made claims as to the possibility of calculating future harms and required therefore that officials assess the likelihood and degree of threat posed before taking preventive measures, precaution has the effect of licensing pre-emptive action even where it is impossible to know what precise threat is posed (Gardiner 2006).

In the field of security, the logic of precaution drives an increasing 'demand for governance of the unknowable' (Power

2004: 40–1) and fuels a consequent desire to 'collect data on anything that is possible regardless of its relevance to the real risks the organization is supposed to be addressing' (Ericson 2007: 13). This logic stands behind proposals for mass surveillance, mass data collection and data retention, passenger name record (PNR) data collection, and biometric IDs, all of which are designed to observe everyone everywhere (Lyon 2007a).

The precautionary approach in criminal justice is analogous to the concept of pre-emption which is well developed in the field of international relations (Sofaer 2003, Shue and Rodin 2007). Pre-emption similarly seeks security in the face of uncertainty by licensing action in conditions of threatened but unpredictable grave harms (Bothe 2003, Dershowitz 2006). One consequence of the war on terror has been to erode the distinction between seeking security on the international stage and the pursuit of domestic security as a task of national government. Serious crime, transnational and organized crime, and terrorist activity interconnect and are seen by the new security specialists to pose an increasingly undifferentiated threat. The international relations discourse of 'anticipatory self-defence', 'pre-emptive strikes', 'rapid-fire justice', and 'deterrence' has come to be deployed in relation to crime control quite as readily as to military intervention (Braithwaite 2006).

Pre-emption stands temporally prior to prevention of proximate harms: it seeks to intervene when the risk of harm is no more than an unspecified threat or propensity as yet uncertain and beyond view. 'Incalculability' and 'radical contingency' are central currency of what Aradau and van Munster term 'governing at the limit of knowledge' (Aradau and van Munster 2007). This imperative to govern even where knowledge is most scarce displaces risk calculation to place the precautionary approach as the dominant driver of current trends in crime control and anti-terrorism policy

(Stern and Wiener 2006). Although it may be the most serious threats of serious organized crime, sexual depredation, or terrorist activity that are invoked to justify preemptive measures, it is clear that this approach is rapidly percolating downward to govern responses to lesser crimes and lesser threats.

Given that the precautionary approach to security constitutes a shift away from the reactive post-hoc orientation of blame and punishment, it might be thought to open the door to non-punitive forms of intervention. Shearing and Johnston recognize this possibility when they ask: 'Is it possible to widen justice within the context of governance of security in ways that uncouple it from punishment?' (Shearing and Johnston 2005: 33). Yet the distinction drawn in law between precautionary measures and punishment has not resulted in retreat from hard treatment and there is little ground for confidence that preventive measures operate non-punitively. If we consider the examples of preventive detention or of preventive orders, it is clear that neither the lack of proven culpability on the part of the individual nor the declared lack of punitive intent on the part of the state results in measures that are any less burdensome or punitive in their effect (Zedner 2007b). If intrusions into civil liberties and hard treatment are common characteristics of purportedly precautionary, preventive measures then it is doubtful whether the onset of the security society renders criminal justice any less punitive (Morse 1998).

As Garland and others have observed, criminal justice policy continues to swing between 'defining deviance down' and an expressive or 'hysterical' response to threat that manifests itself in recourse to punitive rhetoric and draconian penalties (Garland 2001: 131–5, O'Malley 1999). Despite the aspiration that a risk orientation might temper the populist preoccupation with punishment, there is little evidence that these new preventive developments have eroded punitive sentiment. Incarceration plays a large and growing role in the provision of public protection (Zimring and Hawkins 1995, Hudson 2003: 75–6). The public, egged on by a populist press, tend to overstate their collective need for protection and demand that punitive sentences, well beyond those justified by risk, be imposed on those deemed 'monstrous' (Simon 1998, Pratt et al. 2005). Less and less is the prison an instrument of punishment, still less reform, but a carceral warehouse for confining those deemed to pose the highest risks (Simon 2000). As a result, incapacitative and preventive sentencing results in long-term and indefinite prison sentences that push up the prison population to record levels. Mass incarceration may be driven by the economic imperatives of the industry in crime control (Christie 1994) but it is also increasingly central to the security complex.

For example, in Britain under the Criminal Justice Act 2003 those convicted of violent and sexual offences may be held beyond the tariff period of their sentence indefinitely under Indeterminate Public Protection (IPP) orders on the basis of risk assessment alone. The scale on which the IPP order is being used dwarfs the use of conventional fixed-term sentences for serious offenders[4] and has led to a significant rise in the prison population. Incapacitative or protective sentences are now common features of many sentencing regimes and serve to legitimate prison terms far in excess of proportionality by reference to the future risk allegedly posed by dangerous, violent, sexual, or would-be terrorist offenders. Security thus appears capable of radically reconfiguring the uses to which even core criminal justice institutions like the prison are put.

CONCLUSION

These changes in the orientation, values, and organization of crime control so alter the means of controlling crime that they topple traditional models for analysing criminal justice (Brodeur and Shearing 2005). Existing criminal justice principles and values fit ill with the pursuit of security. The classical models of the criminal process developed by Packer, of crime control and due process (Packer 1968), have limited relevance to preventive endeavours operating prior to or even outside the criminal justice system. Core criminal justice principles, not least the presumption of innocence, are threatened by the pursuit of security (Ashworth 2006) and even institutions firmly within the system, such as policing and sentencing, are being reconfigured to new preventive or security-centred ends. Although the engine of human rights seeks to shore up fundamental due process protections, it has also inadvertently had the effect of fostering the development of civil preventive measures not bound by the protections of the criminal process.

In sum, the values with which we have historically sought to evaluate, regulate, and reform the criminal justice system are stretched to their limits by the changing conditions of the security society. Developing new principles by which to govern the pursuit of security or, more ambitiously still, seeking to carve out a new 'jurisprudence of security' (Farmer 2006) is a vital task to which we will return in the final chapter.

5

SECURITY AS INDUSTRY

INTRODUCTION

The previous chapter explored the ways in which the pursuit of security is changing the scope and compass of criminal justice. The present chapter explores the growing provision of security by private and commercial organizations and in so doing revisits the question of whether security is inextricably a state function. Looking beyond the state, it reveals a sizeable and rapidly growing private security sector that provides and sells security products and services for profit. Private security is a burgeoning industry and the technological paraphernalia of security products scatter our social world (Jones and Newburn 1998, Lyon 2001). This industry has played an important role in expanding the scope of security, in creating a market in security provision, and a commodity of security itself (Krahmann 2008). The growth in commercial provision challenges the enjoyment of security by all as a public good (Loader 1999), while diversification and privatization of security services erodes the role of the state as its primary provider and guarantor (Loader and Walker 2001, 2007). At the same time, state security actors are increasingly coming to behave like their commercial counterparts, selling their expertise and services around the world.

The 'marketization' of security results in private security clubs or contractual communities (such as gated communities and private leisure facilities) and virtual communities of credit and insurance. It results in uneven distributions that create marked differentials in provision, leaving some cocooned in security bubbles and others largely outside protection. The state's avowed monopoly over public policing is eroded by the multiplication of security providers. The result is security pluralism or an extended policing family of civilian, volunteer, and private agents. Though much is made of partnerships and community policing, the market for crime control is a highly competitive one, driven by price as much as quality, and in which profit is a more powerful motive than performance.

Some scholars welcome changing patterns of security distribution as permitting local communities to develop their own capacity for self-governance and to meet their particular security needs (Shearing 2006). Others resist it, defending security as inalienably a public good that only the state can properly guarantee (Loader and Walker 2007). They see the commodification of security, its private provision and trading on the market, as inimical to a fully social conception of security that resides in collective public provision and mutual guarantee. And yet the fact remains that the role of the state is being overshadowed by the growth of private provision: public police are outnumbered by private security staff by about 2 to 1 in Britain, by 3 to 1 in the United States, by 5 to 1 in Hong Kong, and between 5 and 7 to 1 in South Africa (Johnston 2006: 33). Notwithstanding the global nature of the security industry, there is striking variation in its penetration of different jurisdictions, with Russia and South Africa heading the list of those countries with the highest private to public police ratios in the world (Johnston 2006), though the security situations in these countries obviously make them special cases.

Despite superficial similarities in terms of role and practice, private security providers generally have different methods and goals to those conventionally sought by the criminal justice system (though see Rigakos 2002). The burgeoning of this industry has profound implications therefore for security as a public good and for wider conceptions of justice. Crudely put, public policing prioritizes the maintenance of norms, social order, and the protection of the public at large. By contrast private security is distinguished 'by its emphasis on a preventative approach to the protection of assets and the maximization of profits' (Shearing and Stenning 1981: 210). Private security is about satisfying the personal demands of those who pay, ensuring a continuing return upon investments, and keeping shareholders happy. It has little interest in upholding the rule of law, providing authoritative expressions of common values, or ensuring social solidarity.

DRIVERS OF THE PRIVATE SECURITY INDUSTRY

Private security is hardly a new phenomenon. Mercenaries are as old as war itself and before the establishment of professional state police and national armies protection for profit was the norm (Percy 2007). Although the past two hundred years have been dominated by the state monopoly on security that is the modern criminal justice system, this may better be understood as a historical blip in a longer-term pattern of private markets in security. In the eighteenth century, prior to the formation of the modern police: 'the market for private gain in crime control was extensive, innovative, and elastic. It was driven by the provision of rewards, immunities, and exemptions' (McMullen 1996: 89,

1998: 99). In this sense the present expansion of private security can be seen less as a new development than as the rebirth of a historically well-established pattern of provision (Johnston 1992, Zedner 2006d).

Much energy has gone into identifying the causes of the rebirth of private security. According to a seminal article by Shearing and Stenning, a key driver of private security provision is the proliferation in the post-war period of 'mass private property', as exemplified by shopping malls, airports, leisure parks, and university campuses (Shearing and Stenning 1981: 240). The growth of these large-scale private recreational, industrial, and commercial complexes shifted more and more from public life into privately owned domains. Notwithstanding their quasi-public status and usage, these spaces are policed by private security services for the purposes of restricting public access and maximizing profit (Shearing and Stenning 1981: 228–9, Button 2003). To the enclosures that sparked the mass private property thesis, new forms have been added, most importantly the growing rash of gated communities of homes enclosed, fortified, and sometimes patrolled against external threats that are now common across North America (Blakely and Snyder 1997, Low 2003) and in parts of South Africa. The result is that 'people are now more likely to be living, working, shopping, and spending leisure time in places which are protected by private security rather than the public police' (Jones and Newburn 1998: 105).

This said, the 'new feudalism' which Shearing and Stenning identified as the natural consequence of the proliferation of private space in North America is, as yet, by no means a universal phenomenon. Some forms of mass private property are becoming more widespread in Britain but they are much less common across continental Europe. As a result the growth of the private security industry, the ability of the market to rival state provision, and the fracturing of state power that this implies is more geographically varied than the mass private property thesis implies. Jones and Newburn observe a tendency to exaggerate the extent and impact of mass private property (Jones and Newburn 1999). Furthermore, they question its explanatory force by cautioning that mere historical coincidence between changing property relations and the rise of private security should not be confused with causation. The growth of private security may therefore require other explanations, especially in those jurisdictions where mass private property is not yet common.

Other motors of the private security industry include high and, in some cases, increasing levels of serious crime. Even when recorded crime levels began to drop in many jurisdictions after the mid-1990s, public concern about crime continued. Economic restructuring and fiscal restraint may also have been significant causes, particularly where that retrenchment appeared to increase crime or decrease the state's capacity to control it. Changes in formal and informal patterns of social control also created a vacuum readily filled by the private security industry. In post-war Britain, for example, the informal guardianship formerly provided variously by park-keepers, caretakers, railway guards, and bus conductors declined (Jones and Newburn 2002: 139–40). In many countries the expansion of the female labour market removed women from the home where they had acted as natural guardians against property crimes (Garland 2001: 82–4). Aside from these push factors several 'pull' factors also played an important role, not least the development of the electronics industry which generated new security technologies such as alarm systems, CCTV, and other monitoring devices (Aas *et al.* 2008). In addition to these 'factorial explanations', Johnston identifies various macro-sociological explanations – not least the rise of managerialism in public service, the spread of market-based forms of service delivery in the public sector, the rhetorical appeal to community, and the impact of globalization – as particularly important in the growth of private security (Johnston 1999a: 180ff).

A larger set of explanations still can be found in the dominant political mentality of neoliberalism. Fostering competition is part of an ideological commitment to the creation of a market society 'in which the pursuit of private gain becomes the dominant organizing principle of social and economic life' (Currie 1997: 147). Neoliberalism both emphasizes the role of individual self-reliance and responsibility for protection of personal interests and, at the same time, promotes risk taking and entrepreneurship as necessary features of the free market. This simultaneous need to manage risk but also to promote risk taking in search of profit is a central tension that is rarely addressed in the larger literature on security (though see O'Malley 2004b).

An important political assumption of the criminal justice state was that risks should be efficiently distributed and that social insurance was the most effective means of ensuring that those least able to bear the burdens of loss would receive some measure of public protection from them. Citizens were asked to have faith in state provision and in effect to cede protection to official hands. Prudentialism redefines security as being once again a matter of individual, communal, and corporate responsibility. Risks are made the subject of private insurance to be bought and sold in the market (O'Malley 1992, 2001). One reason why the state has been forced to retreat in this way is that, by setting crime as a central platform of their political mandate and by responding to populist demand for more punitive sentences, successive governments created for themselves a fiscal and political black hole. The assumption that taxation would provide a sufficient base to fund crime control was dented by increasing recognition of the limits to state resources. The costs of so burdening the tax-payer fostered a political willingness to see others share the burden of these responsibilities. Faced with the spiralling costs of social insurance, the state began to promote personal responsibility and, with it, private insurance. On one reading, therefore, the rise of private security is a product of the fiscal crisis of the modern state and 'the changing structure of the capitalist economy and changes in the organizational form of capitalist enterprise' (Spitzer and Scull 1977: 22).

As the state has increasingly relinquished its role as underwriter of the hazards of modern life, the insurance industry has acquired a central place in the security story (Ericson *et al.* 2000). Insurance companies provide incentives for investment in security measures through reductions in insurance premiums; they require corporate and private clients to purchase security equipment and services as a precondition of insurance contracts; and provide advice, propose service providers, police take-up, and monitor the quality and servicing of installations. The sheer scope of this expansion is illustrated by the fact that subscribers to private alarm centres in the Netherlands grew 1100 per cent in the fifteen years to 1998 (van Dijk and de Waard 2001a). Whether and to what extent prudentialism is driven also by increasing intolerance of risk and desire to protect or insure oneself against harm is an open question to which we will return (Hughes 1998). One paradox of the growth of insurance is that the industry itself may generate its own security risks or 'moral hazards'. Insurance cover reduces incentives to avoid risk or take preventive security measures, and may even encourage risky behaviour by policy holders and third parties that increases the chances of loss since they are secure in the knowledge that it will be compensated (Ericson *et al.* 2000: 537). In order to regulate the consequent moral hazards and minimize fraudulent claims, the insurance industry has generated substantial surveillance and security technologies that in turn become market commodities in their own right.

Deprived of the safety-net of welfarism, the individual under neoliberalism must buy these security products, take out insurance, and assume responsibility for their own welfare in order to mitigate the risks that inevitably accompany life in the market. Yet as Stenson has observed, 'prudential techniques are exclusive rather than inclusive ... they involve a greater reliance on commercial insurance for home insurance, security services and so on and they also involve a narrowing of the communities of risk sharers, excluding those deemed to be unreliable, dangerous or too poor' (Stenson 1996: 109, Young 1998, Ericson *et al.* 2003). If private security is impelled mainly by external political and social factors it is fostered also by new sources of consumer demand.

SECURITY CONSUMPTION

Consumer culture reconfigures security as a commodity to be supplied and consumed like any other. The pull of consumer demand is quite as important as the exogenous drivers of the private security industry, not least because the growth in private property ownership and personal wealth means that consumers have greater capacity to buy (Johnston 1999b: 179). An obvious possible cause of increasing consumer demand is the growing sources of insecurity that feed individual anxiety and public fear (Johnston 1999b, Newburn 2001). At the micro-level, insecurity results from anxieties about personal safety and the vulnerability of property. As Neocleous observes, ' "insecurity" comes to be used as an ideological strategy for encouraging investment in private health care schemes, private pensions, and the commodities that are said to make us more secure, turning us into consumers of the products of finance capital and the security industry; (in)security is nothing if not big business' (Neocleous 2007a: 37).[1] Although there is considerable research on fear of crime, little work has yet been done on the correlation between personal insecurity and security consumption. Until more research is undertaken, it is difficult to say why people adorn their homes with security devices and burglar alarms (Loader 1999) or why communities, government agencies, and commercial businesses increasingly buy in surveillance, patrols, door guards and other security services.[2]

Several possibilities suggest themselves. In respect of personal consumption, security is bought because people can afford to do so; because they have so internalized the 'responsibilization' strategies of governments (Garland 2001: 124–7); and consider it their duty so to do. They may buy security goods and services because they add value to their property or, as insurability becomes the norm, because doing so is a requirement of their insurance contracts or reduces their premiums. Security products may also prevent consumers from falling behind their more security-conscious neighbours. The caché of the prominent alarm signals, at little cost, that the home is a wealthy one and that the owner has the means and sense to protect it. Nor does it seem too far-fetched to suggest that gated housing developments rely upon calculations by developers along very similar lines (Blakely and Snyder 1997, Low 2003). The gated community (arising as it does most commonly in middle-class, low-crime areas) is less a direct response to crime than a positive selling point signalling a certain quality of life and, quite literally, exclusiveness. Security consumption by corporate bodies is bigger business still and driven by a wide array of factors from internal risk audits (Power 2004); to the demands made by insurers (Ericson and Doyle 2004); and to the desire to maximize the sense of security enjoyed by clients in inner-city business districts, leisure environments, and shopping centres in order to maximize profits (Newburn 2001). A less easily verifiable factor might be the desire by companies to protect the intangible asset of their corporate reputation, especially in the context of scandals surrounding Enron and Arthur Andersen that led to new regimes for corporate governance. Here resort to private security provides for covert, internal solutions to corporate malfeasance and crimes against the company, avoiding negative press attention and the attention of public auditors (Gill and Hart 1999).

At the macro-level, there is a considerable literature on the lack of public confidence in the state that may underpin demand for greater private security; though this too remains speculative. Pavarini argues: 'An unfulfilled need for social security generates a social demand for security . . . the crisis of the social state has coincided with the emergence of security as a burning political issue . . . This is no temporal coincidence: there is a structural link' (Pavarini 1997: 79). He argues that the demand for security is less a response to crime than the symptom of a larger crisis within the social state. This analysis is suggestive but it begs the question of why it is that these larger social anxieties have coalesced around issues of security and personal safety.

One possibility, suggested by Bauman, is that the demand for security results from a 'transfer of anxiety' (Bauman 1998: 116) effected by governments cynically well aware that they can do little about the larger sources of insecurity. Governments recognize that they have little control over major threats to individual and communal security such as global warming, economic instability, and long-term unemployment. Instead, by promising to fight crime they hope to condense larger anxieties into concern about safety, in the sense of safety of the body and of property, alone. As Bauman observes: 'in an ever more insecure and uncertain world the withdrawal into the safe haven of territoriality is an intense temptation' (Bauman 1998: 117). By promising safety of the person and the home, governments hope to obfuscate larger sources of anxiety and thus conceal the limits to their powers of protection. Bauman's analysis is, in a sense, more sanguine than Pavarini's in that he conceives this tactic as operating effectively to governments' electoral advantage. Where Pavarini sees the growth of private security as a vote of no confidence in the state, Bauman sees both the state and private enterprise as thriving on its ability to exploit anxiety: 'A lot of tension accumulates around the quest for safety. And where there is a tension, political capital will surely be spotted by bright investors and expedient stockbrokers' (Bauman 1998: 117). Bauman's analysis partially explains why the public and private spheres have found themselves in competition for the market that is security.

Decoupled from the ontological risks of crime, security products and services are also sold not only as means to protection against harm but as enhancing individual well-being, social welfare, commercial success, and financial confidence. As Neocleous observes: ' "Security" has become a positional good defined by income and access to private protective services, a prestige symbol concerned less with dealing with the social causes of insecurity and more with one's own private safety and personal insulation' (Neocleous 2007a: 37). 'Shopping for security' is a significant form of modern consumption. Consumers are encouraged to exercise their choice to buy protection where and in what measures they please. The problem for the burgeoning security industry is that security consumption has 'a powerful in-built capacity to disenchant' (Loader 1999: 381) as security products inevitably signal the risks they pretend to repel and amplify disappointment when they fail to protect. Similarly, Davis also speaks of the self-perpetuating market in private security as 'generating its own paranoid demand' (Davis 1990: 224). The resulting distributions are determined by market forces rather than by political will or local need

(Johnston and Shearing 2003: ch. 5). To the extent that consumers of private security effectively exit from participation in public security provision, this withdrawal marginalizes and depoliticizes public policing and security. Personal security consumption thus has fascinating, though as yet little explored, implications for individual identity, for social relations, and for the health of geographic and political communities.

THE SCOPE OF PRIVATE SECURITY SERVICES

The result of the twin pushes and pulls of security demand is a shift from the comparatively stable technology of the criminal justice system to the more fluid, flexible and often transient operations of the private security industry (Zedner 2006a: 268). Evidently state structures are not replaced or wholly eclipsed by the emergence of private security. The state no longer appears as the dominant player in the production of crime control but instead as one among many. To the extent that the state's own workings are challenged by the diverse activities of non-state actors, it too becomes noticeably a more fluid and changeable entity than was once the case (O'Malley 1999). State agencies engage in partnerships with local, communal, and commercial collaborators, entertain sponsorship by private firms, and contract out public services to private clients (for example, the policing of football stadia).

At the international level the boundaries between economic interests and national security are blurring even more markedly. Public police and state security agencies have become active players in the global security market from counter-terrorism down to urban crime control. State expertise in democratic policing and conflict resolution has become a valuable export commodity. Take for example the manner in which the public policing model developed in Northern

Ireland has been commodified and marketed as a global brand – the 'Northern Irish Policing Model' – in countries as diverse as Bosnia, Kosovo, Ethiopia, Gaza, Palestine, Jamaica, Guinea, Estonia, New Zealand, Iraq, and Hungary (Ellison and O'Reilly forthcoming). Meanwhile transnational security companies have assumed increased responsibilities for state security; most visibly in Iraq, though this is only part of a much larger picture (Gill 2003: 275, O'Reilly forthcoming). In the emerging transnational marketplace for security, therefore, the relationships between state and corporate players are increasingly complex and the line between public and private ever more difficult to draw. The resultant hybrid forms of 'state-corporate symbiosis' or 'grey policing' further blur the distinction between public and private.

Analysing the size and scope of the private security industry is difficult not least because there is considerable disagreement about which services constitute security operations and whether one should count only bespoke contract security or also include 'in-house' security staff whose security functions may be embedded in other tasks. There is also a tendency on the part of the industry to exaggerate its own size and importance. Part of the complexity arises because the modern security industry is deeply reliant on corporate capitalism and is primarily a service industry for the commercial sector, trading in specialized services aimed at preventing and reducing the security problems associated with mass industrial production and international financial capital (Spitzer 1987). At the international level there is also ambiguity about the ambit of security and whether it extends also to risk-management services, business intelligence, private security consultancies, private military services, and multinational corporations who offer security only as part of a larger portfolio of services (Singer 2003, Avant 2005, Johnston 2006, O'Reilly and Ellison 2006, Lynch and Reilly 2007).

With these caveats about the reliability of figures, it is illustrative to note that the UK industry body, the British Security Industry Association (BSIA), estimates that there are over 75,500 people working in the British private security industry and that total turnover of BSIA member companies was £4.33 billion in 2006. Private security industry turnover in respect of CCTV has risen from £84 million in 1993 to £509 million in 2005, and there are now estimated to be over 4.25 million CCTV cameras in operation. Turnover in respect of manned security has risen from £530 million to £1.575 billion over the same period.[3] Figures for North America are even more striking, not least because the Department of Homeland Security has generated an enormous increase in spending on security. It is estimated that the US security market generated $29.1 billion in revenue in 2006 from 'the threat of terror', of which about 70 per cent came from federal, state, and local government contracts, and current estimates suggest that this will double by 2010.[4] In Australia estimates suggest the private security industry generates revenues of approximately $4.5 (Australian) billion per year and employs over 150,000 security personnel.[5] And according to a study by the Freedonia Group: 'The world market for private contractual security services is projected to expand 8.3 percent annually through 2006, approaching $120 billion.'[6] Contested though they are, these figures suffice to give a sense of the vast size and rapid expansion of the private security industry. Arriving at more reliable figures is rendered impossible by the difficulties of defining definitively what constitutes a security service and by the transient nature of many of the businesses involved.

Security is a diverse industry ranging from tiny one-man guarding operations to multinational corporations employing tens of thousands (Jones and Newburn 1998, Wakefield 2003). Some sections of the security industry are very volatile and are marked by high levels of entry and exit (manned guarding is a good example). Profit margins are generally very low with the result that contracts are fiercely contested. Yet a few players are highly successful, vast global conglomerates like Group 4 Securicor, which has over 530,000 employees worldwide,[7] and Securitas AB, which employs over 250,000 personnel in more than thirty countries and claims a 12 per cent market share of the world guarding business.[8] These large players dominate the global security market. Seeking to exploit market opportunities, expand turnover, and maximize returns to their shareholders they engage in a steady round of takeovers and mergers that result in huge corporations each with enormous turnover, power, and political clout. The result is an increasing bleeding between the different sectors of transnational security as commercial conglomerates buy up private military companies, security technology companies, and security consultancies and provide a growing range of services including secure transport services, security systems, event security, and security services to governments.[9] As yet research findings are only beginning to emerge on the influence of these conglomerates on policing at global, national, and local levels.[10]

Far more typical are the small-time operators with fifty or fewer employees who make up the majority of the firms (Jones and Newburn 1998: 80). These range between door guards or 'bouncers', as they are aptly tagged in Britain (Hobbs *et al.* 2003), who control access to commercial premises, most often in the leisure sector, and other security guards who maintain public order and protect property for businesses, retail outlets, and, increasingly, in residential areas. Undertaking diverse patrolling, transit, and guarding functions they are the public face of the security industry, signalling their presence in deliberately distinctive uniforms and heavily armoured vehicles.

By contrast the covert sphere of the private financial security sector is largely hidden from view (Williams 2005a). Both public and corporate clients employ accountants, lawyers, private investigators, and computer analysts to provide security against corporate fraud, money laundering, benefit fraud, copyright and trademark infringements, and so on. In the private sector financial security entails 'a unique form of customized corporate justice, explicitly tailored to the needs and interests of the paying client' and remote, therefore, from the 'larger moral project, tied to the public interest and the production of criminal convictions' (Williams 2005b: 330). In this sphere crime is no more than a threat to profit margins and law a resource to be managed in the interests of limiting adverse publicity and minimizing exposure to financial risk.

Another security sector entirely is the growing involvement of private security firms in both civil and military security raising the spectre of a new 'military-industrial complex'. The rapidly expanding role played by private military firms in many developing countries has been considerably augmented by the opportunities created by the war on terror and the conflict in Iraq. In 2003 one in every ten people deployed in the Iraqi war were employed by private military companies (PMCs); by 2004 there were 20,000 private personnel employed by 60 different PMCs (Avant 2005: 2–3). The potential problems of accountability and injustice that arise as a result of these developments are aggravated by the questionable power of the state to assert control or to regulate the private security industry (Chesterman and Lehnhardt 2007, Percy 2007). Ironically a historic unwillingness even to acknowledge the existence of private military companies and a deep-seated unease about their role, particularly in weak, transitional, and troubled states, have inhibited the development of regulatory frameworks, leaving the field wide open to unscrupulous operators (Singer 2003).

The dispersed and highly differentiated nature of private security should not surprise. Private security is by nature entrepreneurial and springs up where opportunity arises. The range of operations reflects the variety of vested interests and demands that drive the industry. The result is that the security field is made up of diverse operations with little in common other than the deceptive unifier of the moniker 'security' (Neocleous 2000a).

THE COMMODITY OF SECURITY

Determining what exactly is on offer when security is put up for sale is more complex still. The commodity of security ranges between the symbolic and the material. Much security provision is concerned with providing the appearance and assurance of protection (Crawford and Lister 2004, Innes 2004). The millions spent annually on security derive in large part from the desire of private and corporate consumers to cocoon themselves and, in the case of commercial enterprises, their customers in an apparently safe environment, as much as from any determination to reduce crime rates. The purchase of security products and services by companies within business districts and retail outlets is thus arguably as much about providing consumers with highly visible reassurance that it is safe to linger, spend, consume, and do business as it is about crime control (Huey *et al.* 2005). Security is also a form of relational consumption: each corporate actor must ensure that its conspicuous security provision is at least on a par with its competitor; otherwise it risks losing consumer confidence and business advantage.

The commodity of security also connotes a growing range of material goods from surveillance hardware and computer technologies to the advanced military armoury and combat personnel provided by private military companies. There is so little in common between the domestic burglar alarm and the armed mercenary that it is questionable whether it is useful even to think of security as a homogenous commodity. The picture is further complicated by the fact that the commodity of security is inextricable from the development of new technologies that both drive and are driven by the market for security. Private security has fostered developments in burglar and car alarms, security lights, electronic gates, and other such defensive barriers. In addition to the historic repertoire of manufacturing, retailing, and installing locks, bolts, and bars, the private security industry has also been responsible for considerable advances in technological hardware such as surveillance systems, CCTV, and satellite-tracking devices, as well as more amorphous forensic and actuarial tools, security computer software, and security management systems (Lyon 2007b). In turn technological innovation has driven the market in new security products. Some of these arise from perceived new threats (an example here might be anti-virus software as first line of defence in computer security); others from the very fact of techno-logical possibility (a prime example might be the anti-theft device of SmartWater[RM]).[11] Security thus underpins and is underpinned by the development of a vast array of technologies, of which the CCTV camera is perhaps the best documented and most controversial (Norris and Armstrong 1999, Goold 2004, Aas *et al.* 2008).

The commodity of security thus has an expanding life as a focus of private initiative, commercial venture, and rapidly expanding consumerism. Historically, security tended to be 'primarily defined in negative terms . . . is said to exist when something does not occur rather than when it does . . . when stores are not robbed, pedestrians are not molested' (Spitzer 1987: 47). By contrast, the modern security industry sells its product as desirable in its own right, to be sold, bought, and consumed as a sought-after good. This positive re-packaging of security is remarkable: more and more products are promoted as 'security-enhancing' and sales of goods as diverse as mobile telephones and sports utility vehicles (SUVs) are augmented by their claim to protect their purchasers (Simon 2007: 201). As Valverde has observed, 'the broader debate about "security" has been conducted from the start as if we all knew what security is and where it can be purchased' (Valverde 2001: 88). The selling of security proceeds apace as security is reduced to a product traded in the marketplace.

And yet it remains far from clear that consumption of security actually has the desired effect of making people feel more secure. As Ericson observes, '[s]ecurity is marketed within a system seen as having limitless potential and this system therefore augments insecurity. As with all forms of commodification, the more one experiences security products the more they become objects of desire and insatiable appetite' (Ericson 1994: 171). Paradoxically, the more security products and services people buy, the more they depend upon these purchases to feel safe and the less inclined they are to trust their environment and those around them (Spitzer 1987: 50, Zedner 2003b: 163): hence the proliferation in the United States of 'drive thru' fast-food outlets which do not even require one to leave the safety of one's car. Yet the impossibility of cocooning oneself utterly through security consumption is nicely captured by Simon: 'there is always a moment when a person must get out of an SUV or walk out of an airport or hotel or shopping mall' (Simon 2007: 203).

THE AIMS OF PRIVATE SECURITY

Much of the debate about private security focuses on the number of private versus public employees or the size of the private security industry relative to state provision. Such discussion tends to assume that the rise of private security simply entails private operatives performing analogous functions to those carried out by the public police but for different client groups. It is arguable, however, that the security product on sale by the private sector is quite unlike that historically proffered by the state. Private security offers different kinds of protection, has a different operational logic, different goals, and different measures of success. Private security is less about order maintenance or the upholding of norms than about satisfying consumer demand, providing reassurance, minimizing loss, and, above all, maximizing profit (Rigakos 2002: ch. 5, Prenzler and Sarre 1998: 2, Wakefield 2003). Pursuit of the profit motive may coincide with the demands of crime reduction, but may equally lead in quite other directions. The imperative to conceal company losses suffered through employee fraud, for example, militates against the public revelation that prosecution would require (Williams 2005a). Instead the perpetrators are quietly dismissed, left free to continue their depredations elsewhere.

Agents of the security industry are interested less in punishing the wrongdoer or restoring order than in averting or recovering losses. Their principal interest is to identify the sources of opportunity for wrongdoing, to harden targets, to minimize future losses, and secure restitution for past ones. By making the provision of security financially profitable for those who invest in it, the industry hopes that their products will, at very least, appear to pay for themselves. The growth of private security signals not merely a transfer of authority for crime control. Rather it presages a more radical shift from criminal justice and punishment to protection and loss reduction (Shearing and Johnston 2005: 32) and an even more fundamental shift from the maintenance of norms to the maximization of profit.

This can be seen most clearly in the field of security against financial crimes, an arena in which state resources were always limited; state investigative and prosecutorial capacity a subject of ridicule; and the criminal process, and trial by jury in particular, patently inadequate to the gargantuan task of unscrambling and prosecuting complex, transnational financial frauds. The model of a shift from public to private sector policing does not adequately describe the very different culture, practices, and objectives that apply to private financial security services (Williams 2005a). These can better be seen as emergent spheres of security provision supplying financial and other services aimed primarily at protecting assets from depredation, the appetite for which is met by specialist non-state suppliers trading in settings over which the state never had nor claimed an effective monopoly.

THE ECONOMICS OF THE SECURITY MARKET

Private security is promoted on the grounds that the market provides more efficiently than the state; that it is more responsive to consumer demand; and, most contentiously, that private security consumption by the rich frees up state resources for the protection of the less well endowed. Notwithstanding these claims, there are a number of reasons to doubt the desirability of a free market in security.

As we have seen, a few vast players tend to dominate the security market. This raises questions about the feasibility of open competition in an arena where sunk costs, economies of scale, and track record tend to privilege existing contract holders over competitors. In a few cases the creation of these market monopolies appears to be a deliberate (if usually covert) aim of governments, especially where privatization or contracting out is a political imperative but the vagaries of the market pose too great a risk of instability. Sometimes it is an open policy. For example, in France the Ministry of Defence created a company to ensure the inspection and surveillance of French nuclear sites but headed it with senior police and army officers (Ocqueteau 1993: 118). Apparently the imperative to privatize is not always sufficiently powerful to overthrow the residual sense of the state's responsibility for matters essential to the safety of its citizens. Longitudinal analysis of privatization programmes, contracting out, and the independent development of private security providers would further reveal the tendency of the security market to oligopoly. While the existence of an oligopoly is not inconsistent with competition and may even enhance efficiency, the security market is characterized by further ills that place in question its ability to thrive. A flourishing market requires that there be genuine competition, that contracts are enforceable, and that consumer choice is well informed. Problems such as competitive breakdown, information deficits, and incomplete coverage are so common in the private security sector that reliance upon the market is problematic even within the logic of economic rationality.

Security conceived as a commodity is a good explicitly on offer only to those with the power to purchase. Its distribution is unequal as private providers protect the partisan interests (whether individual, communal, or commercial) of those who pay. No surprise here: it is central to the logic of market societies that goods be distributed not according to need but to the ability of the consumer to buy. The market thus transforms security into what economists term a 'club good'. Club goods are excludable but non-rivalrous, allowing them to be supplied in ways that make them 'collectively available to members of the "club" but where non-members' permanent access to the good can be wholly or partially denied, controlled or charged' (Buchanan 1965, Hope 2000: 86). Purchasers of security tend to be propertied, articulate, able to mobilize themselves, and ready to defend their interests. Those with greatest need of protection are often least able to muster the necessary resources; most likely to be excluded from communal initiatives; and hence to suffer the displacement effects of not being so protected (Hope 2000). Research suggests that where security is distributed according to the ability to buy, the result is growing inequality of protection (Loader 1997b: 386, van Dijk and de Waard 2001b) There is also evidence that inequalities in the distribution of security are amplified by the displacement effect caused when criminal activity shifts from well protected areas to those without protection. Securing an exclusive commercial environment such as an inner-city business district may be conducive to maximizing commercial turnover but have displacement effects that bear heavily on neighbouring 'unsecured' environs (Rigakos 2002).[12]

A key issue therefore is that protecting security as a public good to which all have access is endangered by its promotion as a club good, access to which is limited by the capacity to buy. In the distinction between public good and private commodity the source of provision is arguably less important than the question of access (Coase 1974). Yet limiting access is the very means by which much private security is provided, for example in business districts, gated housing complexes, and university campuses. These 'clubs' are by definition exclusive, creating negative externalities for those outside (Hope 2000: 86, Crawford 2006b). Economic analysis suggests that one means of limiting these burdens is to force suppliers to internalize the externalities they impose and so to absorb some of the costs that would otherwise be borne by those outside the club.

REGULATION OF THE PRIVATE SECURITY INDUSTRY

The powers granted to private security agents, the scope of their activities, and the terms under which they compete with one another and with the public sector vary considerably from one country to another. There appear also to be striking differences in the regulatory framework of requirements imposed (or self-imposed) upon security providers to conform to industry services standards or legislative codes (van Dijk and de Waard 2001b). Requirements as to recruitment criteria, safeguards as to identity, past criminal record checks, and stipulations as to training, uniforms, equipment, and possession of firearms all vary markedly by country. Despite this variation, it is clear that the employees of private security concerns are in general subject to weaker regulatory strictures than are their public sector counterparts.

The relative lack of regulation has profound implications for the quality of the security services on offer (Stenning 2000). Notwithstanding its promise to sell security, ironically the industry is often better known for the dangers it poses to the safety of people and property than for their protection. In Britain the security industry is characterized by rapid staff turnover, high customer churn, and low profit margins, not least because, unlike personal security consumption, corporate investment in security is often a 'grudge purchase' made only to satisfy the requirements imposed by insurance contracts. Private security operatives often have criminal histories, are badly paid, inadequately trained, and of poor quality. Some are drawn to working in the security sectors of guarding, patrolling, and cash transit precisely because it furnishes access to illicit markets in drugs and stolen goods or because it is possible to run protection rackets on the back of legitimate security contracts (Hobbs *et al.* 2002: 362, Lister *et al.* 2001: 365). Hence the rather extraordinary statement from the British government that 'the citizen may justifiably seek some form of assurance that he or she is no more under threat from private security personnel . . . than if they were police officers'.[13] Corruption, violence, trafficking, extortion, and other illegalities are commonplace in the rough trade of door guarding, security patrols, and transit (Singh 2005). But lack of accountability and the erosion of the public interest are no less a problem in the more covert sphere of financial security, where financial impropriety, negligent accounting practices, and inadequate legal advice result in security failings of a different sort. Occasionally, in the case of large public scandals like Enron, these come to light; more commonly financial improprieties are suppressed, losses are concealed from shareholders, and the security of the paying client is bought at the expense of others (Williams 2005b: 327–8).

Given that it is unlikely that the highly profitable security market will wane, developing the means to manage it is an essential first step to contending with the realities of the security society (Zedner 2006a). Since the private security industry fulfils, even usurps, functions historically assumed to be the subject of state monopoly, it is perhaps surprising that the state has been slow to regulate. Until relatively recently, states have relied upon industry self-regulation (though bodies like the British Security Industry Association) and upon the self-regulatory capacity of market competition. On the one hand it is arguable that regulation is not reducible to state legislation. Epithets such as the regulatory society or 'regulatory capitalism' seek to capture the distanced role governments now play in 'steering' or governing at a distance (Jordana and Levi-Faur 2004, Levi-Faur 2005). On the other hand, the failings of private security industry, outlined above, are indicative of a larger 'crisis of club regulation' that calls into question the capacities of the private sector and the market for self-regulation. Moran identifies the 1990s as ushering in an era of 'hyper-innovation' in regulatory governance (Moran 2003: 6–7) that fits well with the proliferation of formal regulatory frameworks to govern the private security industry. For example, in Europe, of 25 EU member states 12 have introduced new or renewed regulations since 2000.[14] In Britain under the Private Security Act 2001, the state Security Industry Authority has been established with responsibility for setting standards and ensuring accountability in private security provision. Whether state regulation of the private sector has been a success is less clear and what constitutes successful regulation is more contestable still, since ensuring the financial success of the security market is by no means the same thing as ensuring the promotion of security as a public good. To a worrying extent private security appears to have acquired the culture capital of legitimacy within the neoliberal order that valorizes its endeavours and renders it resistant to effective regulation.

CONCLUSION

The expansion of private security has undoubtedly altered the scope and orientation of security provision, promoting the pursuit of profit over the upholding of norms and the maintenance of order as the key indicia of success. Yet it is far from clear that private provision has reduced the ambit of state provision. Although privatization has been promoted as a way of shrinking government, in respect of penal policy it has tended to have the opposite effect – expanding rather than contracting the scope of state policing and social control (Feeley 2002: 322). It may be that the relentless selling of security by both private and public agents has fuelled demand so as to expand the market for services. At the domestic level, as Simon observes: 'the fortress-like strategies adopted by many Americans who can afford to invest in their personal and family security erode trust and lead to more reliance on both criminal self-help . . . and on state coercion' (Simon 2007: 277). While at the international level, the global security industry continues to grow apace;

state security agencies compete and cooperate with commercial security companies; and new alliances are emerging that blur the public/private divide.

If there was any serious danger that the state risked being eclipsed by the expansion of private security provision, that risk was in one single day averted by the events of 9/11, the effect of which was to launch what became known as 'the war on terror' and to reclaim for the state a dominant role in the provision of security against terrorist threat – to which we turn in the next chapter.

6

SECURITY AND COUNTER-TERRORISM

Terrorism, and the measures taken by security services against it, once stood firmly outside the precincts of criminological scholarship. In the wake of the attacks on New York and Washington, DC in September 2001, and subsequent attacks in Bali, Madrid and London, that changed rapidly. The radical changes brought about by the new threat of global terrorism, by anti-terrorist measures brought in to counter that threat, and the expanding role of the security services all became subjects of criminological enquiry (Walker 2004, Deflem 2004). This is hardly surprising, for the new security policies have had significant knock-on effects on criminal justice values and practice and the subsequent development of criminal policy (Valverde 2001, Walker 2004).

It is doubtful whether it was ever plausible to segregate entirely issues of national security from those of domestic and community safety. It is certainly no longer possible to do so. In the post-9/11 landscape the distinctions between external and internal security; between terrorist threat and serious and organized crime; between anti-terrorist measures and crime prevention; and between security services and the police have begun to break down (Deflem 2004, Stuntz 2002). The pressure on governments to think and act pre-emptively against the catastrophic risks of terrorism has led to many developments that blur the line between crime control and security. It has accelerated the trend towards mass surveillance, significantly expanded the scope of inchoate criminal offences that target acts preparatory to terrorism, and led to a host of other anticipatory endeavours in and outside the criminal justice system. At the same time, everyday crime control decisions are made with one eye to their consequences for the state's ability to combat the most serious of criminals. The consequent ratcheting-up effect places greater onus on officials to avert risk and endows them with ever greater powers with which to do so.

COUNTER-TERRORISM AND SECURITY POLICY

The rise of the private security industry discussed in the previous chapter has tended to erode the dominion of the state. In striking contrast, the effect of terrorism is to enlarge state power through anti-terrorist legislation, the proliferation of security measures, and increases in security budgets and personnel. Nowhere is that more evident than in the legislative flurry that followed 9/11 in the United States – not least the creation of the US Department of Homeland Security, a consolidation and extension of many existing government departments into one super-department charged with defence of the American homeland. Thomas observes that the events of 9/11 'profoundly affected the American psyche' and '[p]olitical seismic shock waves reverberated around the globe' in its wake (Thomas 2003: 1193). The need for governments to be seen to 'do something' in the wake of large-scale terrorist atrocity was immense and had the effect of overriding established political conventions and political and legal processes (Cole 2004: 1755).

Of course, terrorism is not a new phenomenon and many states have long-established anti-terrorism or security statutes designed to furnish their governments with the powers needed to tackle it. The activities of the Irish Republican Army (IRA), Basque separatists (ETA), and the Red Army Faction (RAF) in Germany have long since prompted the introduction of special powers and even emergency security measures. Some countries like Israel, South Africa, and Northern Ireland have lived under the shadow of political violence for decades. The difference is that, whereas these sources of threat were generally regarded as constituting a regional or domestic problem, post-9/11 terrorism has assumed global proportions and appears to pose a more generalized threat (Lepsius 2004: 438, Mythen and Walklate 2008: 223). The scale and severity of recent attacks have created a widespread consensus on the need to strengthen the legislative armoury and stimulated a frenzy of law making such as to generate what Gross identifies as 'an alternative system of justice' aimed at dealing with suspected terrorists (Gross 2003: 1011). In part this is driven by a sense that the conventional tools of criminal justice failed to prevent the security catastrophe that was 9/11. As Braithwaite observes: 'One of the failings of the FBI before September 11, 2001 was that they had limited interest in intelligence that would not help secure prosecutions – their regulatory strategy with terrorism was far too preoccupied with one, preferred tool – prosecutions' (Braithwaite 2006: 106). This perceived failure has prompted the development of alternative tools and procedures that deliberately sidestep the constraints and protections of the criminal justice process.

International organizations like the UN, the European Union, and the Council of Europe have played a limited but growing role in developing international protocols on anti-terrorist policies. Through a series of resolutions, the UN Security Council has defined terrorist acts as a threat to international peace and security, thereby making its decisions directly binding upon member states. Resolution 1373, adopted on 28 September 2001, contained detailed binding rules on the legislative measures to be adopted by states (Nuotio 2006: 1005). Under this resolution, the Security Council required all member states to criminalize terrorist financing; freeze certain funds; criminalize terrorist acts as serious criminal offences domestically; and impose proportionate punishment. It also led to the establishment of a separate Counter-Terrorism Committee to monitor the implementation of the Resolution and required all states to report to the Committee on steps taken to implement it (Nuotio 2006: 1006). In general, states with previous experience of domestic terrorism managed to conform to these requirements more readily than those with none that had to implement much larger-scale reform very rapidly.

Likewise, in June 2002 the European Union adopted the Council Framework Decision on Combating Terrorism, requiring member states to take prescribed measures against terrorism by the end of the year, just six months after it was adopted. While the Framework Decision played an important role in prompting EU member states to define terrorist offences and develop appropriate security policies, provision for national discretion led to considerable variation in the speed and implementation of policy locally (Nuotio 2006: 1010). That said, provisions for joint intelligence gathering and information sharing, common investigation and policing ventures (not least under Europol), and the elimination of extradition proceedings for terrorists combine to ensure that the European Union plays an important role in the security strategy of its member states.

International protocols and endeavours, together with the larger pressure of domestic politics, have led to a steady stream of counter-terrorism policies in many Western countries. In the months following 9/11 America, the United

Kingdom, Canada and Italy rapidly introduced new anti-terrorist legislation, to be followed shortly after by Australia, Hong Kong, Indonesia, India, and New Zealand (Roach 2004). That initial governmental action has been followed up by a continuing stream of new legislation prompted in part by the further attacks in Bali, Madrid, London, and elsewhere. Governments have brought in a raft of acts instituting draconian security policies.[1] These new laws were prompted by the shared sense that the continuing threat of catastrophic risk required the introduction of powers adequate to meet the security needs of a fearful populace. Legislation has been aimed both at introducing new preventive security measures and at amending and tightening existing criminal law and procedure. Despite a historic commitment to safeguarding civil liberties in countries like France, the executive has invoked its considerable powers to bring into effect plans to counter major security threats through the deployment of police and military resources. Even countries like Germany, Italy, and Spain, which for reasons connected with their recent history of authoritarian regimes have been reluctant to enhance state power, have acted to expand security measures against terrorism. For example, the German Parliament has passed a number of anti-terror statutes, not least the Suppression of Terrorism Act 2002 (*Terrorismusbekämpfungsgesetz*) (Safferling 2006: 1156), which considerably extend state power. In some countries this process has gone so far as to entail basic constitutional reform. For example, in Italy new constitutional principles have been developed to recognize 'security as a right in and of itself and not only as a pre-condition for enjoying other rights' (Patane 2006: 1179).

STATES OF EMERGENCY AND
EMERGENCY POWERS

The capacity of terrorist attack to generate terror and, in so doing, radically to alter the political landscape has been the subject of considerable academic attention. There is a strong sense that these are not 'normal times' or, in the words of US Vice President Dick Cheney, that the contemporary terror has created 'a new normalcy' (quoted in Cole 2004: 1773). What once were hailed as important constitutional guarantees come to be seen as hindrances to effective security. When the stakes are sufficiently high, so the argument goes, commitment to the constitution and the rule of law ought not to become 'a suicide pact' with the state (Dinh 2002: 14, Posner 2006). As Lowe observes: '[e]xceptional anti-terrorist measures are justified by the exigencies of the current emergency as temporary derogations from the normal rules' (Lowe 2005: 195). Aside from the losses to life and property, the strong sense that Western liberal democracy itself is under attack only fuels bellicosity and tends to unify Western nations around the division between 'a civilised, democratic "us" and a barbaric, undemocratic "them" ' (Tsoukala 2004: 21).

Characterizing the fight against terrorism as a war has rapidly become a defining feature of the new security scene (Feldman 2002, Cole 2003, Golove and Holmes 2004, Roach 2005, McCulloch and Carlton 2006). The 'war on terror' provides immediate justification for the introduction of security measures that would be indefensible in peacetime. The claim made is that the gravity of the threat posed by terrorism is such that only an all-out fight will allow democratic nations to survive. Suspected terrorists become 'enemy combatants'; trials are replaced by 'military tribunals'; and imprisonment by preventive detention without the prior requirement of proof of wrongdoing (Cole 2003, Lowe

2005). The indefinite detention of enemy combatants at the American facility at Guantanamo Bay is only the most extreme manifestation of practices being plied elsewhere (Rose 2004). Under the banner of the war on terror, draconian powers are enacted hastily and with little debate. Ordinary sources of opposition fall silent for fear of being charged with failing to take the situation seriously, of undermining national unity, or suffering political fallout should further calamity occur (Thomas 2003: 1199ff). The claims of war thus provide a dual licence to governments greatly to expand the scope of their responsibility and requisite powers and, at the same time, to invoke new administrative measures and procedural channels to pursue terrorist suspects outside the constraints of the criminal process (Zedner 2007c).

This widespread licence to suspend normal rights and protections raises the thorny question: when and in what degree is it justified to conceive of counter-terrorist security policies as a 'war'? (Katyal and Tribe 2002). Feldman asks: 'Is terrorism crime, or is it war? What conceptual framework will or should the United States use to conceptualise its fight against terror?' (Feldman 2002: 457). The question is not merely academic. Which framework or label is adopted has profound ramifications for the choice of security laws and measures introduced in consequence. These ramifications are categorical; that is, they determine whether security is sought through domestic law enforcement channels, through military measures, or as a matter of national security. They are also normative; that is, they determine the legitimacy of the measures consequently adopted. Yet it is far from clear if the war on terror could be won or what it would mean to declare victory. Since the threat of future attack always persists, Ackerman acknowledges that 'if we choose to call this a war, it will be endless' (Ackerman 2004: 1033). This is all the more true since those invoking the term 'war' typically also implicitly reserve the right to determine when the war has ended in such a way as to stifle meaningful discussion about time limits. Given the dubious credentials of claims as to war, it may be that terrorism requires the formulation of new categories. As Golove and Holmes conclude: '[i]nter-national terrorism is obviously neither war nor crime in the traditional senses of those terms. It is rather some combin-ation of both, or perhaps an altogether new phenomenon' (Golove and Holmes 2004: 3).

THE NORMALIZATION OF SPECIAL POWERS

The claims of war and declarations of a state of emergency are most plausibly made in the immediate aftermath of terrorist attacks. As these recede in time, recognition that the threat posed by contemporary terrorism is ongoing undermines any justification for the introduction of emer-gency powers. The very notion of an emergency is premised upon the idea that the threat is likely to be short-lived. If the threat is a permanency, then in what sense can it be justifiable to talk of war or to invoke a state of emergency?

Mistrusting the language of war and emergency is impor-tant for two reasons. Not only does it license significant increases in state power in the immediate aftermath of terrorist attack, but also special security measures designed to deal with emergency situations are often extended beyond the moment of supposed crisis. Despite the inclusion of 'sunset clauses' requiring that these powers be time-limited, experience suggests that they tend to be repeatedly renewed into de facto permanency (Sim and Thomas 1983). Excep-tional security measures become normalized, 'making extra-ordinary powers part of the ordinary discourse of government' (Ackerman 2004: 1041, see also Hillyard 1994, Dyzenhaus 2001). Moreover, the exigencies of combating terrorism come to inform the day-to-day thinking of criminal justice officials and legal actors so that the worst-case scenario is always in mind when the limits of law are under review.

Powers introduced against external enemies also tend to spill over into everyday domestic security domains. Measures whose introduction was justified by the most serious of threats come to be seen as more widely applicable. Instituted originally against terrorists, they infiltrate ordinary criminal law and procedure and are applied to those suspected of much lesser crimes (Gross 2001, Stuntz 2002: 2157). In Britain, for example, reorientation around security has exposed domestic crime control policies to the impact of global terrorism to a degree not seen even at the height of the 'Troubles' in Northern Ireland and the IRA bombing campaign on the mainland.

As Tsoukala observes, 'emergency rules become thus part of an ordinary model of governance, are diffused into the ordinary legal system' (Tsoukala 2004: 21). For example, limits on the right of silence for suspects in respect of interrogation and cross-examination (introduced under the Criminal Evidence Order Northern Ireland (1988) in response to terrorist attacks by the IRA and the hampering of counter-terrorist measures by the refusal of suspects to cooperate) were later introduced into the ordinary criminal process in Britain under the Criminal Justice and Public Order Act 1994. Prolonged beyond the period of the emergency and expanded far beyond the terrorist activities that spawned them, limitations on the right of silence now apply to all criminal suspects in Britain. As Gross points out:

> we should (but rarely are) also be aware of the danger that exigencies may lead to a redefinition, over time, of the boundaries of groups, even those which were deemed well defined in the past, making certain members of the original 'non-terrorist'

group into outsiders against whom emergency powers may be 'properly' exercised.

(Gross 2001: 47)

Where anti-terrorist legislation is widely drawn and the very definition of terrorism so expansive as to capture a broad range of political activity, the more immediate danger arises that new security measures will find wider application against ordinary criminals who pose a far less serious threat (Stuntz 2002: 2157ff). The process of normalization is in effect circumvented by legislative provisions that, motivated by the difficulties of predicting future threats, abandon the pretence that draconian new powers are aimed only at known terrorist suspects (Fenwick 2002: 727). The potential target group extends well beyond any known terrorist organization to a larger population whose risk to the security of the state is less clear. Anti-terrorist security measures subject ordinary citizens to electronic surveillance, mass data collection and retention, searches of their persons and property, identity checks, and a host of other intrusions upon their liberty now become so deeply embedded that they scarcely any longer merit notice (Lyon 2001, Aas *et al.* 2008).

Each new terrorist atrocity prompts legislation adding new and more extensive powers to old, often in apparent ignorance or disregard of existing powers. This incrementally generates ever more draconian measures with which governments attempt to persuade themselves and their voting public that they remain effective.[2] In time public opinion so acclimatizes to extensive security measures that these become normal and unremarkable features of everyday life (Hillyard 1994). If exceptional security measures are not to endure and become normalized, then a wider 'culture of justification' needs to be fostered to ensure that new developments are not merely legal in the narrow sense of satisfying the procedural requirements of being lawfully enacted but that they also satisfy the rule of law substantively (Dyzenhaus 2007: 141). And sunset clauses (by which exceptional security measures are time-limited and subject to mandatory review before renewal) need really to see the sun set on emergency powers unless there are very good reasons for their extension.

UNCERTAINTY AND THE 'UNKNOWN UNKNOWNS'

One obvious reason for the development of expansive and widely applicable measures is that security services operate in conditions of considerable uncertainty. How to maximize security in the face of inadequate intelligence is a central quandary for contemporary governments. The former US Defense Secretary Donald Rumsfeld famously observed:

> There are known knowns. These are things we know that we know. There are known unknowns. That is to say, there are things that we know we don't know. But there are also unknown unknowns. There are things we don't know we don't know.
>
> (Donald Rumsfeld, US Department of Defense News Briefing 2002)

Although his speech was widely derided at the time, it is arguable that it articulates the important place occupied by uncertainty in the security field and is in fact a philosophically respectable set of claims despite its sound-bite presentation. Whereas the risk paradigm promised, but could not deliver, reliable calculations about the likelihood and severity of future threats, advertence to uncertainty acknowledges that the future is unknowable. This acknowledgement imposes upon politicians and policy makers the burden of deciding what measures to take and what policies to develop in respect of the 'unknown unknowns'. Security was once predicated upon knowledge 'in the sense that security functions as knowledge, relies on knowledge, produces knowledge, and uses its claim to knowledge as license to render all aspects of life transparent to the state' (Neocleous 2007a: 37). All this is changing: recognition that counter-terrorism necessarily takes place under conditions of imperfect information places uncertainty, not knowledge, centre stage (Ericson 2007: ch. 1, Zedner 2008b).

The 'new terrorism', as it is commonly known, comprises amorphous, transnational terrorist networks about which information is scarce and less easily reduced to categorical suspect populations. It follows that security policy can no longer plausibly rely upon risk assessment and management. Unsurprisingly therefore risk has given way to a larger and more pressing preoccupation with how to manage uncertainty (Aradau and van Munster 2007: 93). Uncertainty can productively be understood as resulting from two distinct sources. First, there is actual uncertainty as to the nature, likelihood, scope, or target of a particular threat and second, fabricated uncertainty caused by the unwillingness or inability of states to adduce evidence. In respect of security, uncertainty may arise both from the unknown nature of the terrorist threat and from the secrecy that, it is said, necessarily attends the operations of security services. Due to the difficulty of adducing sufficient evidence for prosecution, the need to protect operatives and their informants from the dangers attendant on disclosure, and to ensure the continuing efficacy of their operations, intelligence services are often loath to reveal what they know and still less willing to put it to test in open court. Uncertainty here is in an important sense manufactured by the privileging of covert operations and the protection of security service personnel.

Conventionally security policies have been developed by calculating the risk of future harms and requiring officials to assess the likelihood and degree of threat posed before taking preventive measures. Yet, as Power observes: 'the management of uncertainty is inherently paradoxical, an effort to know the unknowable' (Power, 2004: 59). Acknowledgement that the future is uncertain, and in a real sense incalculable (O'Malley 2004a: ch. 1), could translate into fatalism warranting inaction. It is precisely to overcome the tendency to fatalism, particularly in the case of catastrophic threats, that uncertainty has been recast so as to permit pre-emptive action even where it is impossible to know what precise threat is posed. As we saw in Chapter 4, the precautionary approach is just one such attempt to deny officials the luxury of inaction by insisting that lack of full scientific certainty shall not be a ground for inaction in the face of serious or irreversible threat. In the case of terrorism the prospect of catastrophic attack does not appear to permit cautious or prudent policy making but seems rather to demand 'pre-cautious' pre-emptive measures taken even in the face of uncertainty.

LEGISLATING FOR UNCERTAINTY

New terrorist networks lack hierarchical command, they are diffuse, transnational, and diverse in their organizational structures. Recognition that Al-Qaeda is less an organization than an ideology inspiring emulation makes it more than usually difficult to predict who poses a risk. Together these factors render conventional intelligence targeting of known terrorist leaders and hierarchies inadequate to the task. This difficulty is seen to justify intelligence-gathering tactics that rely not only on profiling, and targeting, but also employ mass surveillance mechanisms, like communications data retention, passenger name record (PNR) data collection, and biometric ID that regard everyone as potential subjects of suspicion (Maras 2008). No longer need one be identified as a suspect terrorist to find oneself subject to these security measures. The US Patriot Act 2001 provides the US government with wide powers of electronic surveillance for use in connection with terrorist investigations including suspension of the usual duty to inform targets of surveillance that they are under observation (Roach 2004: 522). The goal of 'total information awareness', as it is called in the United States, is a chimera but in the face of uncertainty it is central to the logic of precaution (Stern and Wiener 2006). Similar powers have been introduced in Canada suspending the duty to inform individuals under surveillance.

In the European Union, where once such mass surveillance was considered unjustifiable, the impact of the Madrid and London bombings has secured its place as an essential plank in the armoury of the war on terror. The European Data Retention Directive (2006) requires all member states to retain communications data pertaining to the traffic between individuals and organizations. Although the retention of such data had long been resisted as incompatible with Human Rights protections (not least Article 8 European Convention on Human Rights (ECHR), the right to privacy – Goold 2007), it has been adopted as an essential tool in the fight against the ill-defined and amorphous threat posed by international terrorism. In Britain the government has permitted data sharing across public and private sectors in order to combat fraud by disrupting the operations of organized criminals (Serious Crime Act 2007, s. 68). Although new special powers such as these are often justified politically by the need to counter the security threat posed by Al-Qaeda, in practice they are by no means limited to combating terrorism.

Beyond surveillance, the precautionary approach underpins a raft of security measures adopted by governments around the world which seek to combat terrorism. This precautionary logic is nowhere better evidenced than in the anti-terror legislation. Here the impulse to govern at the limit of knowledge results in several worrisome tendencies. First, offences are commonly defined in broad, imprecisely defined terms that have the potential to criminalize a very wide range of activities remote from the actual preparation or planning of any specific terrorist act. The US Patriot Act 2001, employs a 'breathtakingly vague and broad definition of terrorism' (Dworkin 2002) and the definition laid down in the UK Terrorism Act 2000 has likewise been condemned as 'immensely broad and imprecise' (Fenwick 2002: 734).

Anti-terrorism laws significantly extend the ambit of criminal liability for association, criminalizing membership of terrorist groups and even peripheral participation in their activities (Roach 2004). For example, in Britain s. 1 of the Terrorism Act 2006 prohibits the publishing of 'a statement that is likely to be understood by some or all of the members of the public to whom it is published as a direct or indirect encouragement or other inducement to them to the commission, preparation or instigation of acts of terrorism or Convention offences'. Indirect encouragement includes statements which glorify the commission or preparation (whether in the past, in the future or generally) of such acts or offences; and from which members of the public could reasonably be expected to infer that what is being glorified is conduct that should be emulated by them. Provided the perpetrator is aware of the risk that the public may perceive it as encouragement, he or she is liable, under s. 1, to a penalty of up to seven years' imprisonment. Anti-terrorism legislation like this overrides traditional limitations in respect of accomplice liability, relying upon the fallacy of 'guilt by association'. It has the effect of significantly expanding the scope of liability, as Tadros observes: 'The direct extension of investigatory powers in relation to the terrorist threat operates in conjunction with this broadened criminal law, permitting raids of premises and stop and search of individuals where the conduct of those individuals is only suspected to be at the very furthest margins of terrorist activity' (Tadros 2007b: 665).

Secondly, inchoate offences are targeted at earlier points in time, remote from commission of the substantive offence or the actual infliction of harm (Roach 2004: 503ff). Again in Britain, s. 5 of the Terrorism Act 2006 criminalizes for the first time 'any conduct in preparation' of the commission of acts of terrorism or assisting another to commit such acts and attaches a maximum penalty of life imprisonment. Furthermore, ss. 6 and 8 make criminal the giving or receiving of training in terrorist activities, and being at a place where training is going on (both of which carry a ten-year sentence of imprisonment). Those apprehended are also made the subject of extraterritorial jurisdiction, so that terrorist suspects can be tried in the courts in the United Kingdom even if committed abroad. These new offences extend even further the range of inchoate crimes established by the Terrorism Act 2000, which include widely drafted offences of possession; of providing financial support to a terrorist organization; of omission; and of supporting, belonging to, or wearing the uniform of proscribed organizations.[3] The combined effect of this anti-terrorism legislation is significantly to extend the ambit of inchoate offences within the criminal law (in respect of Australia, see McSherry 2008). Criminalizing activities remote from the actual commission of an act of terrorism is justified by the need to furnish the legal grounds for action against individuals before the threat posed by terrorism can be realized.

This attempt to develop legal categories upon which to legitimate pre-emptive action in the name of security comes at a cost. The definition of these offences is broad and, at least in the case of terms like 'indirect encouragement' or 'conduct in preparation', extremely vague. The long-established principles of English criminal law that offences be clearly defined and entail acts 'more than merely preparatory' to a criminal offence is here overridden in favour of the unabashed criminalization of indistinctly defined and merely preparatory actions. The 'principle of maximum certainty' (Ashworth 2006: 74), namely that an offence should be clearly defined in law such that an individual can know from the wording of the relevant provision what acts and omissions will make him liable, the requirement of 'no punishment without law' (Art. 7 ECHR), is likewise a fatal casualty of the securitization of the criminal law. Ashworth makes a powerful twofold defence of the requirements of certainty, predictability, and fair warning: first, that 'respect for the citizen as a rational autonomous individual and as a person with social and political duties requires fair warning of the criminal law's provision and no undue difficulty in ascertaining them'; second, that 'if rules are vaguely drafted, they bestow considerable power on the agents of law enforcement . . . creating the very kind of arbitrariness that rule-of-law values should safeguard' (Ashworth 2006: 76). In a striking inversion of these maxims, where security prevails legal precision is no longer deemed a virtue but a hindrance. The pursuit of security in the field of counter-terrorism thus exemplifies what Ericson dubbed 'counter-law' or the proliferation of 'laws against law' (Ericson 2007: 24).

A final consequence of the attempt to develop security policies in the face of uncertainty is the development of new measures outside the criminal process. Where existing constitutional arrangements and procedural protections are thought to be inappropriate to the heightened threats now faced, the tendency is to formulate new structural arrangements explicitly designed to circumvent such hurdles (Günther 2005). One such example is the Control Order, introduced in Britain (and since copied in Australia, Lynch and Reilly 2007) against those suspected of involvement in terrorism in the wake of a House of Lords decision that the indefinite detention of foreign nationals suspected of terrorism was unlawful.[4] In the words of the British Home Office, Control Orders are civil 'preventative orders which impose one or more obligations upon an individual which are designed to prevent, restrict or disrupt his or her involvement in terrorism-related activity'.[5] They impose wide-ranging conditions including extensive curfews; tagging; restrictions on access, for example, to computers or communications equipment; reporting requirements; and limits upon personal associates for a period of up to twelve months at a time (renewable on application to the court) (Zedner 2007b).

The Control Order is thus an extraordinary security measure that does serious damage to basic presumptions of criminal procedure (Bonner 2006). It lays waste to the presumption of innocence (Ashworth 2006); to the right to a fair trial; to adversarial justice; to transparency (not least in its use of closed session and Special Advocates);[6] and to proportionality. It imposes burdensome restrictions without furnishing an adequate basis for challenge or access to the information necessary to test the evidence or to rebut the grounds according to which these restrictions are deemed necessary. Although the order is imposed in civil proceedings there is no need to meet the ordinary 'balance of probabilities' test. It is possible to impose these restrictions provided that the Home Secretary reasonably suspects the individual of involvement in terrorism-related activities and deems the Control Order necessary for the protection of the public. Breach of these conditions is a criminal offence punishable by imprisonment for up to five years (Prevention of Terrorism Act 2005 (PTA), s. 9(4)(a)).

The Control Order thus seeks security by enabling the state to impose restrictions upon suspects without exposing covert intelligence to the public scrutiny attendant upon prosecution. It seeks security even in the face of uncertainty in a number of important ways: the key definitions of 'terrorism' (PTA 2005, s. 1(9)) and 'related activity' are vague and potentially expansive; the conditions imposed are imprecisely set out; and the distinction between restriction of liberty and its deprivation under Article 5 ECHR is nowhere articulated. As Ericson has observed, whereas in law 'uncertainty has conventionally spelled innocence, within precautionary logic uncertainty is a reason for extreme pre-emptive measures for which designated agents are held responsible, and monitored and sanctioned accordingly' (Ericson 2007: 23, McCulloch and Carlton 2006: 404). The Control Order thus exemplifies the willingness to act pre-emptively in the face of uncertainty that is perhaps one of the most striking features of the new architecture of security.

BALANCING SECURITY AND LIBERTY

From all that has been said it should be clear that the pursuit of security against terrorism poses no small threat to the very liberties it purports to protect. A central dilemma of contemporary debates is how to balance security and liberty, and indeed to what extent balancing is a useful metaphor for thinking about the issues involved. The notion of balance is familiar from criminal justice where the interests of defendants versus those of victims or the public at large are set against each other in policy debates, commonly to the detriment of defendants' rights. Criminal justice scholars have warned against the perils of the balancing metaphor and attempted to institute a more rigorous, structured approach to the weighing of competing interests. For example, Ashworth warns that achieving a balance is put forward 'as if it were self-evidently a worthy and respectable goal' whereas it might better be thought of as 'a rhetorical device of which one must be extremely wary' (Ashworth 2002: ch. 3).

Despite such warnings, in the debates on terrorism balancing continues to prevail. Security and liberty are set in a zero-sum game in which more of one is taken necessarily to mean less of the other. Politicians and judges habitually appeal to the notion of balance to justify new security measures or to defend controversial decisions. The threat posed by terrorism and fear of the next attack provides grounds for tipping the balance heavily in favour of security and against countervailing claims to civil liberties. Unsurprisingly, this tendency has spawned a considerable academic literature dedicated to critical examination of the notion of balance and its limits as a tool of policy making in respect of security (Dworkin 2002, Waldron 2003, Zedner 2005, Ashworth 2007, Kostakopoulou 2008). There are several grounds for scepticism.

First, that rebalancing presupposes *an existing imbalance* that can be calibrated with sufficient precision for it to be possible to say what adjustment is necessary in order to restore security. Yet terrorist attacks create a political climate of fear that is not conducive to sober assessment of the gravity of the threat posed (see, for example, Dinh 2002). The well-documented difficulties associated with accurately assessing threats to security ought to act as a check. As I have argued elsewhere, 'If the claimed need to rebalance is not to be a cavalier piece of political dishonesty we need much greater precision in identifying the external factors that may be permitted to tip it' (Zedner 2005: 512). Conditions of high uncertainty do not conveniently mimic the hypothetical 'ticking bomb' scenario of a catastrophe bound to occur if action is not taken and the uncertainty surrounding future threats ought to act as a brake on too ready a willingness to tip the balance.

A second ground for caution is the question of *whose*

interests lie in the scales when rebalancing is proposed. This issue is generally fudged by the implicit suggestion that security is to be enjoyed by all. In practice the balance is commonly set as between the security interests of the majority and the civil liberties of that small minority of suspects who find themselves subject to state investigation (Heymann 2002, Waldron 2003: 201). Dworkin puts it more starkly:

> with hardly any exceptions, no American who is not a Muslim and has no Muslim connections actually runs any risk of being labelled an enemy combatant and locked up in a military jail. The only balance in question is the balance between the majority's security and *other* people's rights.
>
> (Dworkin 2003)

Although the trade-off between the security interests of the aggregate *us* versus the individual *them* is rarely made explicit, the weight of numbers hangs implicitly in the balance to tip it in *our* favour. The purported balance between liberty and security is thus in reality a 'proposal to trade off the liberties of a few against the security of the majority' (Waldron 2003: 194). Even where surveillance and security policies and practices are universalist in conception, they tend to be highly discriminatory in their application, particularly at the hard end of anti-terrorist measures. Claims to rebalance in the name of public protection or national security are laid down as trump cards against which any individual claim to liberty cannot compete. Which leads Dworkin to conclude: 'we must decide not where our interest lies on balance, but what justice requires, even at the expense of our interests, out of fairness to other people' (Dworkin 2003).

Third, claims to rebalance rarely entail a close consideration of *what lies in the scales*. Any talk of balancing implies commensurability, but in practice little consideration is given to the precise rights, values, and interests in play on the side of liberty or the exact benefits to be derived in respect of security. Assigning priority to these competing interests assumes that they are amenable to being weighed one against the other. Yet there are at least two grounds for doubting the commensurability of security and liberty interests. The first is that, as we have already observed, we are weighing collective interests against those of small minorities or individuals. The second is what might be called temporal dissonance, namely the fact that we seek to weigh known present interests (in liberty) against future uncertainties (in respect of security risks). Although the certain loss of liberty might be expected to prevail over uncertain future security benefits, future risks tend to outweigh present interests precisely because they are unknowable but potentially catastrophic. Fundamental rights that ought to be considered non-derogable and to be protected are placed in peril by the consequentialist claims of security.

Together, these concerns should provide a powerful check upon demands to rebalance in the name of security. As Thomas concludes: 'the idea of trading off freedom for safety on a sliding scale is a scientific chimera . . . Balance should not enter the equation: it is false and misleading' (Thomas 2003: 1208). Given the powerful political appeal of balancing, the primary challenge is to find an alternative rhetoric with which to frame the debate and to this end we turn back to criminal justice.

SECURITY, TERRORISM, AND CRIMINAL JUSTICE

One possible means of eschewing balancing as the primary means of determining appropriate security policies is to appeal to the core values of criminal justice, even at the expense of maximizing security. As Dworkin suggests:

We might well be a safer society if we allowed our police to lock up people they thought likely to commit crimes in the future, or to presume guilt rather than innocence, or to monitor conversations between an accused and his lawyer. But our criminal justice system has not evolved through calculations of precisely how much risk we are willing to run in order to give any particular class of accused criminals a certain degree of protection against unjust conviction: we do not give accused murderers, for example, less protection than accused embezzlers or jaywalkers.

(Dworkin 2002)

Willingness to uphold due process protections even at the cost of sacrificing security might be greater if it were possible to ' "de-terrorize" the political atmosphere' (Thomas 2003: 1222), not least by better informing the public of the scale and likelihood of the risks they face. The facts do not substantiate claims that we live in an 'age of terror', as Mueller observes:

Even with the September 11 attacks included in the count, however, the number of Americans killed by international terrorism since the late 1960s . . . is about the same as the number killed over the same period by lightning – or by accident-causing deer or by severe allergic reaction to peanuts. In almost all years, the total number of people worldwide who die at the hands of international terrorists is not much more than the number who drown in bathtubs in the United States.

(Mueller 2005: 220)

Similarly, the death toll from the Madrid bombings only equalled twelve or thirteen days of fatalities on the Spanish roads and that from the London bombings represents just six days of fatalities on Britain's roads.[7] While there is, of course, a special wrong involved in the intentional, wanton killing inflicted by terrorist attack that is not captured by actuarial calculation, a better-informed public might be less demanding of security measures. And yet the difficulty remains that, however successful efforts to inform and to reassure are, it takes only a single atrocity to re-ignite the state of fear that licenses the introduction of new emergency powers and yet more draconian measures.

Meeting subjective security needs by reassuring the public is a legitimate policy goal. But the evidence from criminology is that promoting the reassurance function can have the effect of significantly inflating the role of policing (Innes 2004: 168). Conceding to popular fear of terrorism is likely to be even more expansive and liable to give rise to 'comfort legislation' aimed at maintaining public confidence rather than seeking effective security. History tells that public fear is all too easily deployed to instigate and justify exceptional measures such as the suspension of *habeas corpus* (during the American Civil War) or mass internment (of Japanese Americans during the Second World War) (Sunstein 2005: 204). Where such measures are selective and the mass of the public will not face them, the natural political resistance which ordinarily acts as a political check does not arise (ibid.). In respect of terrorism, adopting measures solely in the service of subjective security is tantamount to allowing terror to drive policy. Instead, before any new security measure is introduced there needs to be 'an actual prospect that security will be enhanced' (Waldron 2003: 209). Security measures that are otherwise unnecessary, ineffective in promoting objective security, or liable to provide fuel to the terrorists' cause cannot be justified by their claim to serve subjective security alone.

Permitting the effective attainment of objective security to determine policy is not unproblematic, however. If a security measure is in principle wrong, then efficacy alone ought not to be deemed to provide a sufficient justification or render legitimate a measure that is unjust. Security measures need also to abide by basic principles of justice. One solution is to insist that suspected terrorists be pursued within the ordinary criminal process (albeit accused of the most serious of crimes) and considered as criminal defendants to whom the principles of criminal justice apply (Zedner 2005: 509, 529ff). Although the pursuit of security in the face of terrorism raises the stakes, this need not take it outside the constraints of the criminal law and the criminal process. So far as possible, terrorist suspects should be prosecuted for substantive crimes and, if found guilty, punished in the ordinary way (Lowe 2005: 188–90, Heymann 2002: 452). The presumption of innocence and the privilege against self-incrimination, access to impartial legal advice and legal aid, rules of evidence, charge with a substantive offence, adequate time and facilities to prepare a defence, the right to confront witnesses, rules against hearsay evidence, and on the admissibility of evidence are all important protections of the criminal process (Thomas 2003, Ashworth 2007). Insisting on the prosecution of terrorist suspects would have the effect of ensuring that they are entitled to these due process protections and would render transparent any departure from them (Tadros 2007b).

The dangers of not adhering to the ordinary principles of the criminal process are well illustrated by the observation by the British human rights organization Liberty that:

> more than 7,000 people [were] detained in Britain under the Prevention of Terrorism Act (1974 to 1992), the vast majority have been released without charge and only a tiny fraction have ever been charged with anything remotely resembling terrorism. Almost without exception these people could have been arrested under the ordinary criminal law.
>
> (Wadham 2002)

Post 9/11 the tendency of the threat of terrorism to erode existing safeguards is even greater and can be countered only by a determined insistence that those accused of the most serious crimes deserve no less protection than those accused of lesser offences. Given that the likely severity of the consequent sanction is much higher, arguably terrorist suspects require even more. Departing from due process is not only unjust, it is also liable to be counterproductive. As Dworkin argues:

> Almost the entire point of any criminal trial – civilian or military – is to decide whether those who are accused of crime are actually guilty of them ... Of any proposed set of procedures, we must ask not whether the guilty deserve more protection than those procedures afford, but whether the innocent do.
>
> (Dworkin 2002)

Dworkin does not, of course, mean to suggest that guilt alone is sufficient. Guilt must be proven according to the law and all the procedural and evidential protections it provides. When disregard for due process results in wrongful convictions, not only are the innocent convicted, the guilty may go free. Security, far from being served, is diminished.

CONCLUSION

One of the ironies of pursuing security is that at the same time as claiming to protect liberty from one source, terrorism, it diminishes the protection of liberty from another, the state. This is a double irony given that, as we saw in Chapter 2, an important strand of classical liberalism has been to protect civil liberties from encroachment by the state. Security properly defined would encompass not only public protection against terrorist threat but also the security of the individual from unwarranted state interference. As

Mythen and Walklate argue: 'If the pursuit of security comes at the expense of human rights, then not only is the quality of that security compromised, but the very principles of democracy are threatened' (Mythen and Walklate 2008: 236). One modest means of resistance would be to re-conceive due process as the rightful protection of the security of the individual against unwarranted intrusion by the state. The larger task of enhancing collective security against terrorism without diminishing the security of the individual from the state remains one of the central problems of our times.

7

GOVERNING SECURITY

INTRODUCTION

From all that has been said thus far it will be clear that one of the thorniest aspects of security is its governance. The changing patterns of security distribution (discussed in Chapter 3) are indivisible from the normative question of its governance (Stehr and Ericson 2000, Johnston and Shearing 2003, Goold and Lazarus 2007, Loader and Walker 2007). This final chapter examines why security is in need of governance; considers various means by which it might be governed; and takes the first steps towards articulating core values for the security society. It examines the claim that the already complex relationship between security and the state is further complicated by the fact that we are now increasingly governed *through* security in the sense that diverse policies are directed towards or justified by the claims of security (Valverde 2001: 89, Simon 2007). New measures, policies, programmes, and strategies, invoked in the name of security, alter the very shape and direction of government. At the same time new sites of security governance in the private sphere and at the communal level alter the landscape of crime control and throw up new challenges for the governance of security as a public good that cry out to be addressed.

THE PARADOXES OF SEEKING SECURITY

A core problem of governing security is that security itself is so powerful an aspiration that to invoke it rhetorically tends to pre-empt critical scrutiny. Security is presented as politically neutral, as necessary, and so obviously desirable that it is not easy to gainsay. The enormous political capital that inheres in the term 'security' means that any policy pursued in its name is virtually unassailable, for how could anyone reasonably be opposed to security?

The consequence is a depoliticizing of security that is inimical to discussion about its proper place in political and social life. Security is commonly asserted as a basic right or fundamental good which has the effect of foreclosing debate about its priority or relationship with other goods.[1] Where security is deemed to stand prior to all other goods (aside perhaps from subsistence), employment, health, and education necessarily take second place. The claims of security budgets prevail, with necessarily detrimental consequences for spending on schools, hospitals, and welfare (Valverde 2001: 89). The capacity of security to license draconian measures is fuelled partly by the impossibility of knowing precisely against which threats security measures must protect. Because the powers demanded by states in the name of public protection brook no easy empirical challenge, security is a powerful rhetorical driver used to push through measures that might otherwise be resisted. Security is invoked as the justification for intrusions upon civil liberties, as well as the ground for mass accumulation, storage, and exchange of information about individuals and organizations. Claims that it is necessary to collect, retain, and share personal data override concerns about privacy rights and data protection. Part of this book's purpose has been to invite critical scrutiny of security in all its myriad forms, to excite suspicion, and in so doing to resist the natural tendency to accept security as a trump card. Considering the costs entailed is an essential task of accounting when security is proffered as the justification for public policy or private venture.

Reinvigorating critical discussion relies on challenging the claims made in the name of security and exposing the problems that beset its pursuit. Let us explore six paradoxes of security which call into question its claim to be an unqualified good and make explicit the challenges thrown up for its governance.[2]

First, although security embraces the pursuit of risk reduction it presumes the persistence of threat. As became clear from the first chapter, security has an unattainable quality, its pursuit can never be said to be over since unknown vulnerabilities, new threats, and new adversaries always leave it open to challenge (Freedman 2003). The threats of crime and terrorism (or famine or environmental disaster), even if reducible, remain ineradicable. The durable quality of these threats renders security an ongoing struggle. More cynically still we might observe that, given the political capital, professional ambitions, and profitable enterprises invested in the security business, it is in no one's interests for risk to be eradicated entirely. Risk is essential to the health of the security market; without it shares would surely tumble. The inescapable conclusion is that absolute security is unattainable and that, even if it were, is not sought by those whose political and economic prosperity relies upon continuing threat.

A second paradox is that the expansion of the private security industry has enlarged not diminished the penal state. Although one might expect the pursuit of security through private endeavour to make possible a corresponding reduction of state effort, it has been accompanied instead, at least in Britain and America, by an unprecedented expansion of the penal state (Braithwaite 2000). And while one might expect pre-emptive security measures to permit lesser reliance upon post-hoc punitive ones, penal politics have not become less punitive. Rather, the rise of security has added to and amplified the role of the criminal justice state. Part of the explanation lies in the fact that punitiveness and demand for security are intertwined (Zedner 2003b: 160–2): penal repression signals a need to protect against threats, and the public respond by seeking out their own measures of protection. The result is akin to a security race between public and private providers. Private security personnel trawl more suspects into the criminal justice system and augment the ambit of state surveillance and control. Furthermore, the need to regulate private security operations adds new layers of regulatory legislation, provision for licensing, inspection, and audit, and so further expands the remit of state control.

Third, although security promises to reassure by improving individual and collective perceptions of safety, ironically the paraphernalia of security tends to raise perceptions of risk, increase anxiety, and to disappoint when the feared risk materializes and the security measures are seen to have failed. Increasing awareness of risk is a necessary facet of encouraging individuals and communities to take sensible precautions and to alter their practices in order to minimize their exposure. Yet it comes at a certain cost. Those who are most vulnerable or least able to take the measures necessary to reduce exposure may feel more insecure than before. Heeding crime prevention advice by avoiding travelling alone on public transport or outside the home after dark may actually increase risks by reducing the natural surveillance that comes with the presence of people. For the private security industry, maintaining a certain level of insecurity is essential to ensuring a continuing market for products, even though these very products promise protection. The scattering of our social world with signs, alarms, and CCTV cameras advertises the risks of crime at every turn with the result that, as Davis observes, 'the social perception of threat becomes a function of the security mobilization itself, not crime rates' (Davis 1990: 224). The more security provision there is, the more it is regarded as normal and necessary, the greater the consequent anxiety if it is not available or one cannot afford protection.

A fourth paradox is that although security is posited as a universal good, its pursuit is predicated upon threat and, therefore, those who threaten. Pursuing security necessarily places some sections of the populace outside protection and entails targeting and incapacitating those deemed to pose a threat (Loader 1997a, Zedner 2003b: 166). Social exclusion is thus an inescapable companion of security, a fact exacerbated by the common tendency to overstate claims for public protection. Whereas punishment applies to those who have been convicted of wrongdoing, security relies on techniques for identifying, classifying, and managing aggregate suspect populations (Feeley and Simon 1994, Feeley 2004). Those so identified are deemed to pose a threat irrespective of any wrongdoing and are liable to find themselves excluded from public, quasi-public, and private spaces on the basis of age, sex, or appearance alone (von Hirsch and Shearing 2000). Dangerous sexual or violent offenders, 'super predators', and terrorist suspects are deemed most to threaten and are prone to be demonized and incarcerated in the name of security (Simon 1998, 2000).

Setting security as an object of policy has the tendency to sidestep the issue of whose security is being sought. The claims of mass public protection when juxtaposed against the loss of individual rights for the few seem overwhelming (Dworkin 2003: 37). Where security is a saleable commodity, accountability to the democratic polity is liable to be usurped by the more powerful demands of narrower constituencies, be they bounded political communities, consumer groups, or shareholders. Since those liable to lose most by security measures tend to belong to politically weak and often hugely unpopular groups such as suspected sex offenders or terrorists, it is difficult to assert their interests without risking political defeat in the increasingly populist politics of the security society. The larger the population likely to benefit from security-driven restrictions and the smaller the population liable to bear the burden of them, the less likely is there to be effective opposition. As Sunstein points out:

> People are likely to ask, with some seriousness, whether their fear is in fact justified *if* the steps that follow from it impose burdensome consequences on them. But if indulging in fear is costless, because other people face the relevant burdens, then the mere fact of 'risk', and the mere presence of fear, will seem to provide a justification.
>
> (Sunstein 2005: 208)

It follows that when security-driven restrictions are directed at pre-identified minorities or otherwise selective groups, others must bear a particular responsibility to protect their interests against unwarranted intrusion. Absent the natural political resistance that arises where infringements upon civil liberties are widely shared, there is often a failure adequately to scrutinize the legitimacy of burdens that fall only on minority groups or sub-populations. Demands for collective security against distant and ill-defined threats tend to obliterate the interests of the individual in security against unwarranted state intrusion. Asking explicitly whose security we pursue tackles head-on the assumption implicit in much rhetorical recourse to security that *we* – an ill-defined larger public – need protection against *them* – an ill-defined predatory minority.

Fifth, although security promises freedom and the liberty of citizens to pursue their individual and collective goals free from injury, harm, or loss, paradoxically it has the strong tendency also to infringe individual liberties. In places of exceptional risk and at times of heightened threat, the claim of security over freedom is most easily asserted and ordinary liberties are least defended. Yet the exceptional security measures once thought necessary only in zones of highest risk (like airports and borders) have spilled over into ordinary life and ordinary places. As we saw in the previous chapter, post 9/11 the threat of terrorism has resulted in a considerable erosion of civil liberties in the name of security (Waldron 2003, Zedner 2005). Liberty-eroding measures introduced in respect of the gravest security threats have a common tendency to be come 'normalized' and extended to lesser threats with lesser justification (Hillyard 1994, Dyzenhaus 2001). The burdens of these measures do not fall evenly, as the security interests of the majority are commonly set against the loss of civil liberties by a minority of people who fall into predetermined suspect groups. Justified in the name of 'rebalancing' the scales between security and liberty, seldom are the countervailing costs to individual rights systematically defended.

The sixth and final paradox is that although security is held up as a public good, the manner in which it is pursued too often tends to erode trust and other attributes of the good society. Many security measures and practices are based upon a presumptive mistrust of strangers and many security technologies (for example, surveillance, data retention, access control, and target hardening) operate further to erode trust by presuming everyone to be a potential source of threat. The proliferation of agents, technologies, and strategies of security both signals and fosters a lack of trust in fellow citizens that impoverishes social relations (Duff and Marshall 2000: 22, Bigo 2000). The pursuit of security not only degrades civil society by creating a climate of generalized suspicion but in so doing is liable to generate demand for more security. It also tends to undermine trust in public institutions which is a major form of social capital in modern democracies. For example, mass surveillance can be seen as a statement by the state to the effect that 'we do not trust you, the public', the answer to which might be 'and so we, the public, cannot trust you the state'.

Taken together, these paradoxes require that the unbridled pursuit of security not go unchecked but instead be justified by reference to clearly enunciated principles. And yet the very idea that security needs special justification is rarely considered. There is a sophisticated literature that recognizes that punishment – as pain inflicted by the state – needs to be justified (Duff and Garland 1994: 2). Granted, the burdens imposed by punishment are, as a class, more serious than those generally entailed by security measures. In general (though not invariably) security measures are less intrusive and less burdensome (though more pervasive) than are the pains of punishment. Nevertheless, in the name of security individuals may be spied upon, subject to searches of their person and property, suffer restrictions upon their freedom of movement, and may even be incarcerated. And whereas those subject to penal measures need to have been found guilty of a criminal offence, those subject to security measures need have no wrong proven against them but only belong to a suspect group or act in ways that invite suspicion as to their future risk. Instead of being sacrificed in the name of security, those so suspected ought to enjoy all the protections that the presumption of innocence requires.

It is thus a moot question why security has not been seen to require special justification or attracted the attention of moral philosophers and political theorists to the same degree as has punishment. The old adage that 'prevention is better than cure' provides some ground for pre-emptive actions. But it does not furnish an either complete or unlimited justification, not least given that governments have introduced significant coercive powers in the name of prevention which do not respect the safeguards ordinarily applicable in criminal cases. If states are to be restrained in their use of preventive powers, a conceptual, normative, and procedural framework is required. While the limits of the punitive state have been explored extensively, the idea of the preventive state has scarcely been addressed either doctrinally or conceptually (Steiker 1998). This lack is beginning to be addressed by a growing literature on the 'jurisprudence of dangerousness' (Slobogin 2003); on the rise of the 'preventive state' (Janus 2005); as well as on the 'jurisprudence of security' (Farmer 2006); but a clearly articulated normative framework has yet to be fully developed.

INSECURITY, RISK, AND UNCERTAINTY

Before we consider the nature of the good that is security and the means to achieve it we ought not to lose sight of the fact that it is possible to have too much of a good thing. Were it not for the threat of release, one might enjoy complete security in the isolation block of a maximum security prison. But maximum security is not a condition without costs. As Davis observes, in America the Los Angeles millionaires 'are hardening their palaces like missile silos' (Davis 1990: 248), while in the LA housing projects conditions are even worse: 'Visitors are stopped and frisked, while the police routinely order residents back into their apartments at night. Such is the loss of freedom that public housing tenants must now endure as the price of "security" ' (Davis 1990: 244). Security also licenses forms of defensive cocooning that are potentially burdensome and, ultimately, detrimental. I can wrap myself and my family in cotton wool, bolt the doors, and bar the windows in order that we be safe, but to what end? We may feel and even be safe but at no small cost to our quality of life.

Although security is commonly sold and pursued as an unassailable good, we rarely stop to reflect upon what a 'security society' or a hypothetical state of absolute security would look like. Supposing for a moment that it were attainable, a state of absolute security might well prove suffocating. For the all the claims to fix the future made by security (Zedner 2008b), certainty is by nature simultaneously static and backward-looking. It rests upon maintenance of the status quo unimpeded by the perils of the unknown. Instead of seeking to immure ourselves in ever higher walls or impose upon our pockets and our liberties ever greater burdens, we need to ask 'how much mutual policing is the protection of the commons worth? (Scott 2000: 43).

The dangers of feeling too secure were not lost on our historic forebears. Historically, subjective feelings of security signified an absence of anxiety that was regarded as culpable in its negligence, an open invitation to harm. Note this usage in *Macbeth*, Act 3:

He shall spurn fate, scorn death, and bear
His hopes 'bove wisdom, grace, and fear;
And you all know, security
Is mortals' chiefest enemy.

Far from being a valued state of mind, security is characterized here as an unfounded confidence, a form of pride before the inevitable fall. By implication, therefore, insecurity was a valued form of prudence. This world-view has long since been overlaid by a desire for security that relies upon false promises by governments and private security companies, and wilful blindness to the facts of crime by individuals. As such, and as I have pointed out elsewhere, it is a puzzle why the myth of total personal safety is so powerful and enduring (Zedner 2000: 203).

The financial and political leverage inherent in security's negative analogue – insecurity – is equally a source of concern (Crawford 2002, Huysmans 2006). Insecurity has come to refer to everything from anxieties about crime, unemployment, financial uncertainty, and personal health, to concerns at the international level about the dangers of climate change, population growth, and terrorism. A populist politics of insecurity licenses exclusionary policies in the name of crime reduction and public protection. These concerns lead some security scholars to declare themselves 'against security' (Neocleous 2000a) or to suggest that we can have 'too much security' (Zedner 2003). One might go further to argue that insecurity, far from being an ill against which all manner of measures are justified, is in fact a prerequisite of Western liberal democracy and a necessary facet of a neoliberal economy (O'Malley 2004a: ch. 3). Certainty is hegemony, it relies upon authoritarian rule. Democracy inevitably creates and relies upon the uncertainty of dissent, challenge, and protest for its flourishing. Western market society is reliant on entrepreneurship, on risk taking, and the exploitation of opportunity. Security, taken to its logical extreme, appears inimical to both.

Risk has positive as well as negative possibilities that tend to be dismissed in writings on security. Risk is opportunity, it is what makes possible the lucky break, the new prospect, and the chance to do. If we are to remain open to chance and to avoid the suffocation of security, even negative risks need to be subject to qualification not elimination. Yet we remain unwilling to entertain the possibility that risk, insecurity, and uncertainty may have positive qualities generally overshadowed by the larger claims of security and certainty. De

Lint and Virta rightly observe that criminology has failed to question the assumption that security is an unqualified good whose pursuit trumps all other goods. Privileging security, they suggest, undermines the value of uncertainty and ambiguity that lie at the heart of political debate and a healthy democracy. Instead, uncertainty is cast alongside insecurity as a problem to be fixed by national security policies that champion necessity, exceptionalism, and emergency powers (De Lint and Virta 2004: 472). In place of the authoritarian tendencies of security, they propose a 'radical security politics' that 'is both a rejection of authoritarianism and an embracing of ambiguity' (De Lint and Virta 2004: 473). Rejecting the conventional association of security with certainty, they find 'security in ambiguity', arguing that ambiguity and uncertainty provide the wellspring of politics and the spur to political engagement that is the necessary bulwark to 'the terror of the unambiguous order' (De Lint and Virta 2004: 480).

In similar vein, O'Malley explores the positive possibilities or what he terms 'the uncertain promise' of risk. He provides an important counter to the belief that the popular demand for security promotes awareness of risk, generating a vicious circle in which greater risk-awareness causes greater insecurity and hence the demand for yet more security (O'Malley 2004b: 325). Instead we might consider Bernstein's proposition that risk is good news: 'we are not prisoners of an inevitable future. Uncertainty makes us free' (Bernstein 1998: 229). Although risk is inherently dangerous, it is arguable that criminology has concentrated too much on its negative side. In order to overcome this negativity we would do well to consider the many and various uses to which risk can be put, not least because so doing reveals risk to be a political construct with both positive and negative possibilities. Learning how to live 'securely with risk' is for Loader an essential first move in resisting the upward spiral of security that otherwise threatens to overshadow debate about the kind of society we aspire to live in (Loader 2008: 407). Developing an 'ethics of risk', as O'Malley proposes (O'Malley 2004b: 334), requires recognition of the varieties of risk in play and therefore the different ways in which risk may be deployed as a resource in the pursuit of 'a democratized, agonic politics of security' (O'Malley 2004b: 338).

THE MEANS AND ENDS OF SECURITY

A final step before we can consider the nature of the good that is security is to address its relationship with other values, interests, and goods. For security is commonly posited as being in tension with other goods. As Valverde observes, 'people seem to think that it goes without saying that if we want to have more security we will just have to lose something from our democratic rights, and that if we decide to hold on to these rights and to our democratic traditions more generally, then our collective security may suffer' (Valverde 2001: 83). Rejecting this Hobbesian view of the trade-off between freedom and security, Valverde insists that 'measures that enhance the security of the state are often inimical not only to the rather abstract freedoms we call civil liberties but even to that fundamental good that criminologists call "primary security", that is, the basic physical security of oneself and one's loved ones' (Valverde 2001: 84). On this view, limiting our collective claim to security is an important safeguard against the loss of security that would result from eroding restraints on state action.

As we saw in the previous chapter, a common response is to set security in the scales to be balanced against liberty, freedom, and justice, from which position it is argued that only by balancing these conflicting interests can security be kept in its proper place. The problem with this mode of analysis is that it does not ask what security is for (Waldron 2003). If instead of seeing security as in tension with these other goods we thought of it as fundamental to them, then any security measure that tended to erode rather than promote their attainment would, by definition, be illegitimate. Rather than seeing security as part of an inherently precarious balancing act set against other goods, security measures might better be understood as justified only insofar as they conduce to their attainment (Zedner 2005).

One persuasive line of philosophical argument is to reconceive security not as an end in its own right but to see its pursuit as justified only insofar as it serves, or is at least compatible with, ulterior goods such as liberty, justice, equality, trust, and social inclusion (Dinwiddy 1978: 21). It follows that it does not make sense to posit the relationship between security and these goods as in tension, still less as a zero-sum game, but rather as properly interdependent (Kelly 1990: 89). Whereas security is generally seen as standing in competition with the protection of individual liberty, on this view the pursuit of security is justified precisely because it is a precondition of liberty. Understanding security this way would lead us to abandon balance and other computational metaphors in favour of a more cohesive conception of security and other goods that 'seeks to integrate the two, to amalgamate them indissolubly' (Lustgarten and Leigh 1994: 9). If, instead of viewing security as a threat to liberty, we regard safeguarding liberty as one of its very purposes, then upholding individual freedoms looks less like the defence of liberty against security than an integral facet of its pursuit. Security here is both the present security of one's person and property and also the security of knowing that one can make plans in the expectation that one has a reasonable chance of fulfilling them. Without security of expectation one cannot make choices about the future.

This re-conception of security recognizes it not as an attainable end goal but as a necessary prerequisite of other goods, from which it follows that it cannot make sense to draw a sharp distinction between ends and means. Duff and Marshall propose an alternative ethical perspective that 'denies that we can always specify the end in a way that leaves open the question of the means thus open' (Duff and Marshall 2000: 20). The ends or goals of security measures need to be specified in such a way as to ensure that the means by which they are sought are consistent with the ends sought. For example, to search your colleagues as they leave your office might secure your book collection but would hardly be conducive to fostering a healthy and trusting academic community. Likewise, where security measures are introduced in the name of protecting individual freedoms, it is illogical to permit them unduly to erode civil liberties – since it is liberty that justifies them in the first place. And to the extent that measures are justified by reference to ontological security it cannot make sense to license measures that in practice induce insecurity. Recognizing that security is less an end in itself than the means to other ends requires new forms of moral reasoning capable of capturing this dualism.

Some of the hard philosophical legwork has already been done in respect of punishment; Duff argues that what makes the punishment an appropriate method of pursuing its justifying goals 'is not, as it is for the consequentialist, the contingent fact of its efficiency as an instrumental means . . . it is the character of the goals themselves. . . . In this context "means" and "ends" are logically, not merely contingently, related' (Duff 1986: 7). Although Duff concedes that it is sometimes possible to distinguish the justice of an end-state from the justice of the process by which it was achieved, he denies that it is possible to 'separate the justice of a conviction from the justice of the procedures through which it was achieved' (1986: 115). Added to which, disregard for civil liberties and the demands of due process may result in wrongful convictions and the acquittal of the guilty (Dixon 1997: 283). The same argument can be extended to security measures: although it might be practically efficacious to prevent terrorism by imposing a blanket curfew on members of suspect populations, the measure would be unjust. What renders a security measure just is that it employs means that can be rationally defended as intrinsically appropriate to the end sought. If security is a prerequisite of freedom for all, it cannot be fair to allow the burden of security to fall on a section of the population in such a way as grossly to impede their freedom. Just as for Duff 'the justice of a verdict is internally related to the justice of the procedures which produce it' (1986: 119), so the justice of a security policy relies upon the justice of the means by which it is pursued. Or to put it another way, the justice of the means is integral to the very attainment of just security.

GOVERNANCE OF SECURITY IN A MIXED MARKET

The changing patterns of security provision discussed in Chapter 3 have profound implications for its governance. Although security has long been the primary task and *raison d'être* of the modern state, its dispersal to multiple private providers transforms the role of the state. Modern governments buy out of direct provision to allow a larger role for private players who are increasingly permitted, even invited, to assume previously core state responsibilities for social order (Stehr and Ericson 2000, Ocqueteau 1993). It remains a matter of debate whether changes in security provision represent the beginning of a larger social transformation (Bayley and Shearing 1996) or whether they are better understood as part of a more gradual, less dramatic trajectory of change (Jones and Newburn 1998).

The challenge of how to govern security in a mixed market of public and private provision is now an important subject of academic deliberation (Johnston and Shearing 2003, Loader and Walker 2004, 2007). Whether the increasingly scattered providers of security are better understood as arrayed in a horizontal market model (Dupont 2004: 79) or in a 'state-centred "vertical model" ' (Crawford and Lister 2004: 426) is a matter of analytical dispute and normative debate about how security provision ought to be regulated. If, as Crawford and Lister argue, the state is more than merely one node among many, its role remains pivotal in respect of both its symbolic power and its regulatory capacity. If, on the other hand, the state is merely one 'node' in an increasingly diverse security network, then the issue is less who governs security than who provides and who has the power to purchase. Shearing argues against a 'state-centred view of governance that excludes, or at least obscures, private governments' (Shearing 2006: 13). For Shearing, statism is objectionable both because it underplays the importance of private governance and, more controversially, because it limits normative thinking. Shearing insists we recognize the state police as but one node or security provider 'among many' (Shearing 2006: 27). Dismissing the Hobbesian account of the state as Leviathan, Shearing favours a residual role for the state as providing the auspices under which security governance is devolved to private and communal providers operating within a free market. Johnston, his frequent co-author, likewise insists 'the state is one player – albeit a crucial one – in a network of governing agencies': this is no mere descriptive statement, for it underwrites a clear normative refusal 'to give priority to any particular locus of power' (Johnston 2006: 34).

Even among those who see the market as increasingly

important there is disagreement about whether the networks between providers, employing horizontal layers of accountability rather than hierarchical rule, or the nodes (or points of provision) are the primary means of governance. Whereas network analysis relies upon claims of coordination between security providers, nodal governance makes no claim as to coordination and gives no set of nodes conceptual priority. Indeed Shearing and Wood positively argue for the need to 'stop giving conceptual priority to state nodes' (Shearing and Wood 2003b: 404–5, Wood and Shearing 2007). Shearing and colleagues applaud the local empowerment inherent in 'community nodes' and see security as best provided from the ground up. For Shearing and Wood, although the emergence of these communal nodes or new 'denizens' can lead to the creation of unwelcome 'governance deficits', they can produce new and potentially beneficial forms of communal self-rule through the enhancement of 'local capacity governance'. Shearing and Wood optimistically contend that, adequately resourced, local community governance can deepen democratic control over the provision of security in ways that are consistent with its provision as a public good. They see the dispersal of security measures as creating spaces of greater civil participation in governance. The language of local capacity building suggests a democratic dispersal of power to local communities, minority groups, and others formerly denied access to or purchase over the formal processes of government.

The possibilities of local capacity building become particularly germane when the state is weak or 'failing'. Dupont and colleagues explore the possibility of transferring mechanisms for the co-production of security from stronger states to those where conventional security mechanisms are either poor or non-existent. They propose new institutional arrangements which, they believe, have the capacity to arrest the decline of security in the least secure nations of the world. Recognizing that blanket policy transfer is unlikely to be successful, they advocate 'value pluralism' capable of adapting to the 'diverse contexts, cultures and knowledges found in weak and failing states' (Dupont *et al.* 2003: 341). Taking the example of innovation in one South African township, they promote the 'Zwelethemba model' of peace-making, peace-building, and partnerships to create sustainable, managed, and regulated 'Peace Committees' charged with local resolution of conflict and the building of local capacity for security (Johnston and Shearing 2003: 151ff). These developments clearly challenge the state's prerogative to resolve criminal disputes by claiming that it is too remote from the community to be able to serve communal interests adequately. Only by returning disputes to the community, it is argued, can the interests of all parties be considered and met. While it is difficult not to be impressed by the courage and creativity with which they actively seek security for those most disadvantaged in the least secure of societies, one might well regard the relatively unproblematic manner in which its advocates present the Zwelethemba model as overly optimistic, even dangerously so.

A less benign reading of nodal governance is possible. Despite the appeal of local capacity building, to govern from the ground up in the name of security raises worrisome issues. First, Peace Committees and other local developments are so dominated by the security agenda that they create the risk that local communities come to be governed through security. Second, ceding the power to punish to community fora introduces the risk of less attractive aspects of informal justice. Vigilantism, the pursuit of private vengeance, and the vilification of particular groups or individuals, whether on grounds of race, social status, or because their particular crime is one abhorred by the community in question or at that time, are all risks potentially associated with community-based justice. The problems of local justice in native communities elsewhere in sub-Saharan Africa, as well as in Australia and Canada, should make one wary of too optimistic a recourse to community-based resolutions of crime or security problems (Roche 2003).

Moreover, instead of being part of the solution, it can be argued that nodes in fact represent points of greatest difficulty in the new organization of security provision. Kemshall and Maguire observe that 'the interface between each organization's accountability structure and those of other agencies is a point of tension as they enter the multi-agency arena. The "seamless join" is often more rhetoric than reality' (Kemshall and Maguire 2001: 257). Rather than seeing nodes as the potential site of governance, therefore, should we rather see them as points of conflict? Do Shearing and colleagues underplay the professional differences and conflicts of interest inherent in the intersection between public and private agencies, between national and local interests, or even within local communities? Certainly the development of local, communal, and private security provision has potentially problematic consequences for democratic legitimacy. Marks and Goldsmith provide an illuminating case study of private security provision in South Africa which furnishes particularly potent evidence with which to question the faith elsewhere evinced in nodal governance as a means of empowering 'the weak to direct their own affairs' (Marks and Goldsmith 2006). As Marks and Goldsmith make clear, promotion of local governance (like the Zwelethemba model of community Peace Committees) relies upon questionable assumptions about the ability of local communities to organize, to accord with the rule of law, and to share and implement a clear moral code. If the extensive critical literature on communitarianism has not alerted security scholars to the dangers inherent in resort to community governance (Crawford 1998), empirical studies such as these surely will.

The frailties of communal governance, the difficulties of accountability and self-regulation impose upon the state the duty to supply regulatory oversight where provision is in local or private hands. As became clear in Chapter 5, successful state control is difficult to achieve not least because formal regulation presumes common purpose, transparency, clearly articulated goals, and a degree of stability, whereas the security market is characterized by wide disparity of provision, divergent goals, and volatility. In other spheres where formerly state functions have been made the subject of market provision – for example, the privatization of prisons – problems of regulatory oversight have already been addressed and provide a potential model. Here regulation has been sought through minutely defined contracts, inspection, and the introduction of new regulatory structures and agents like the office of the prison controller and the prison ombudsman. Elsewhere regimes of licensing, training, inspection, and sanction for non-compliance also provide a template for regulation of security providers. In practice, state governance is often reliant upon regulatory hybrids that depend for their success partly upon the self-regulatory capacity of the security industry or other security providers; partly upon market competition which permits dissatisfied customers to withdraw their custom; and partly upon third-party gatekeepers like the insurance industry to impose service standards on security providers (Kraakman 1986). The difficulty remains that without a clearly articulated common purpose the pursuit of profit (whether financial or political), not protection, prevails.

THE GOOD OF SECURITY

One of the most pressing issues raised by the changes so far described is that of accountability for security as a public good. Where security is sought by agencies in and (more particularly) outside the state the formal channels of democratic accountability become more remote and less effective. The state remains important as the author of statutory frameworks within which public and, to a lesser extent, private security agencies function, but its ability to impose a clear regulatory framework is severely compromised. The consequent dispersal of accountability places greater power in the non-democratic and sub-political hands of interest groups, non-governmental organizations, private agencies, and even consumer groups. This creates for a worrisome dispersal of accountability away from the political to the altogether more diffuse realms of partnership, multi-agency cooperation, and the market.

Since the eighteenth century at least, the notion of security as a public good has been central to the formation and function of the modern state. Not only is it the responsibility of government to provide it, but the pursuit of security actively licenses the exercise of state power. As a basic requirement of human flourishing, the state-centred model of security insists it must be provided for all citizens regardless of their status or wealth. Indeed, as we saw in Chapter 2, the Hobbesian model of the state was based upon a social contract between all individuals who surrender part of their liberties, personal assets, and rights to the 'sovereign', who in turn guarantees their personal safety. As we have seen, the history of recent security politics is riddled with the dilemmas posed by changing patterns of distribution away from the state to private, communal, and local providers. The problem of how to achieve equitable distribution of this basic public good under such conditions is one of the most important issues of contemporary criminal justice.

The issue is complicated by the fact that the preservation of security as a public good is arguably determined less by the source of provision than the question of access (Coase 1974). In crude terms security can be maintained as a public good much more readily in public spaces, whereas in privately owned space protection is necessarily limited to those who have access. In between, the proliferation of localized security provision, such as arises on university campuses, creates 'zones of governance' (Crawford 2003) or 'communal governments' that provide spaces for the development and use of 'common goods' (Shearing and Wood 2003a: 207). A more restricted form increasingly common in North America is the residential gated community (see Chapter 6) whose members buy rights of access to communal services such as maintenance and security enjoyed in common (Blakely and Snyder 1997, Low 2003). In localized, semi-private spaces such as these security might better be thought of as a 'club good' to which only privileged members have access and from which outsiders are explicitly excluded (Hope 2000, von Hirsch and Shearing 2000, Crawford 2006b). As these examples reveal, changing patterns of spatial distribution are thus powerfully determinative of the nature of the good provided.

Thus, although access to public goods is arguably more important than who provides, in practice the expanding non-state provision of security by private corporations, NGOs, communities, and private citizens has the effect of limiting access. Against Shearing's faith that the 'plural project of private governance through markets' can work alongside the state to 'promote the commonweal' (Shearing 2006: 20), Loader and Walker insist that a thicker notion of security renders its collective provision indispensable and the state a 'necessary virtue' in that provision (Loader and Walker 2005). Over a series of works they have articulated a robust conception of security as inalienably a public good and mount a spirited defence of the state as its rightful guarantor (Loader and Walker 2005, 2007). Evidence of fragmentation of security provision does not diminish the responsibility of the state to provide, to regulate, and to call to account. For Loader and Walker, security constitutes an integral part of the rights and goods enjoyed in common that help generate individuals' sense of identity, and the social meaning of security is such as to require democratic governance of its distribution. They therefore insist that security ought not to be thought of as a tradeable commodity subject to free exchange within the market. Indeed the very idea of private security, they argue, is 'oxymoronic'. Building on the earlier work of the political theorist R. N. Berki (Berki 1986), they argue that the 'security of any individual depends in some significant fashion upon the security of others' (Loader and Walker 2005: 185). Considerations of accountability and justice require rather that security be provided within a framework of democratic deliberation and decision making: the role of the state is therefore to mediate the rights of citizens *vis-à-vis* one another's security through laws (Berki 1986).

The claim that our own security is dependent upon that of others has important implications for the channels and instruments by which we pursue it. Acknowledging that my security depends upon your security requires that the means I employ in pursuit of my own safety do not unduly encroach upon your interests and that yours do not trespass upon mine (Loader and Walker 2007). Understood this way, effective security must be security for all. The difficulty is to ensure a realm of security in which each of us is able to exercise the widest possible freedom compatible with the same realm of security for others. Maximizing security therefore necessarily has distributive implications (Rawls 1973: ch. 1). Despite all attempts to transform security into a saleable commodity, conceiving security as a public good means that we cannot envisage, still less provide, security without a clear conception of the public sphere and the role of the state within it.

CONCLUSION: PRINCIPLES AND VALUES
FOR A SECURITY SOCIETY

Though the state can no longer claim a monopoly over security, it can, nonetheless, insist upon its right to delineate and uphold the normative structures essential to protect the public interest in security and to maintain the ligatures of civil society. Despite the proliferation of new security providers that combine to disperse power, it remains the case that law provides the legal framework within which security is pursued, that the state provides for licensing, oversight, and regulation, and that accountability lies ultimately with state governments. As we saw in Chapter 5, industry self-regulation has proved inadequate to the task of weeding out rogue security providers and the self-regulatory capacity of market competition has not proven adequate to the task of maintaining standards. It falls to the state, therefore, to assume responsibility for the regulation of security even or perhaps especially when it is provided beyond the public sphere.

At a time when other disciplines, not least international relations and war studies and, in quite different ways, the biosciences, statistics, psychiatry, and genetics scramble to colonize security as a terrain over which they can claim sovereignty, criminology has an existing expertise in the area that renders it particularly well placed to lead the field. Reducing 'security threats' to matters of crime prevention; insisting that even the gravest prospective harms be tackled with proper regard to due process; and recognizing that security measures, like penal ones, require special justification are just a few of the steps criminologists might take to tame security, capture the field, and reassert the liberal values that lie behind much criminological endeavour. Criminal justice, procedure, and criminal law are also fertile ground from which to harvest appropriate normative structures, regulatory mechanisms, and even models for an overarching 'security authority' or standing ethical committee capable of securing public deliberation, ethical oversight, and accountability in the delivery of security.[3]

An important first step is to consider the limits to security and to set out the principles upon which a framework for security might be grounded. The principle of *necessity* might circumscribe or even inhibit the introduction of security measures that find their justification in sources of minor nuisance or trivial threat. Stipulating a 'threshold test', which the threat posed must meet, would be a further productive first step to delimiting recourse to measures in the name of security. For example, the introduction in Britain of the Anti-Social Behaviour Order (ASBO) permits police, local authorities, and others to obtain court orders upon those who commit anti-social, but not necessarily criminal, conduct that impose extensive restrictions, the breach of which can result in imprisonment for up to five years (Burney 2005). Yet it is questionable whether merely anti-social behaviour is a sufficiently grave threat to security to justify such an intrusive measure (see generally, von Hirsch and Simester 2006). A 'real threat' requirement would oblige policy makers to identify and furnish evidence that without the proposed measure actual harm would result. Given intelligence about future harms is often limited and even where risk is calculable at some level its precise extent is uncertain, this would act as an effective inhibition on unwarranted measures. In respect of grave intrusions, one might also add an 'imminence requirement' to inhibit the introduction of measures aimed at ill-defined, unduly distant threats.

The principle of *minimalism* might further limit excessive responses to minor threats. The burdens imposed by security policies should be kept to the least amount possible and measures used only where lesser methods would not suffice.

In order to maximize the liberty of its subjects, the state should always prefer less intrusive measures (Ignatieff 2004). Mill's model of maximizing liberty is an especially apposite one in the context of pursuing security (Mill 1979). Wherever possible, security should be sought through regulatory mechanisms, such as regulations to make the environment safer and situational controls to reduce opportunity for wrongdoing that do not impact unduly on those subject to them. A 'no alternative' requirement would be that where other, less intrusive means of averting a security risk exist, then these means must be tried and exhausted first. Where less burdensome or less costly measures would suffice, minimalism would require that they routinely be preferred over intrusive or liberty-depriving ones.

The principle of minimalism needs to be balanced against the principle of *social defence*, not least because if the balance is not struck it may lead to the emergence of ad hoc and potentially violent measures of self-defence. If formal provisions for social defence are thought inadequate, people who perceive the need to defend themselves or secure their property will do so or pay others to do so (Johnston 1996). This said, the remote possible dangers of vigilantism, protection rackets, or the Mafia ought not to license resort to security measures in the name of social defence where lesser measures would suffice. The principle of social defence should not be permitted to slide into penal populism nor deployed to justify otherwise indefensible measures on the grounds of reassurance alone. It would not suffice that a policy allowed politicians to claim that 'something was being done'; it must actually have some chance of averting the particular risk at which it is aimed. The pull of social defence might be resisted therefore by an 'efficacy requirement', namely that any proposed security policy or measure must be effective or at least sufficiently likely to bring about the specific end for which it is ostensibly introduced. That said, efficacy alone will not serve to justify a security policy or measure if it is in principle wrong.

Importing the criminal justice principle of *parsimony* would further delimit the scope of new measures by imposing the positive requirement that measures be the least intrusive and least costly necessary to meet the aim in question and in this runs directly counter to the argument that the 'mass crime' of 9/11 justifies more expansive police powers (Stuntz 2002: 2142). Determining whether a security policy or measure is justified according to the principle of parsimony further requires that information pertaining to that assessment be made as widely available as possible. This is important not least in order to determine its larger political, economic, and social consequences and to make an informed assessment as to whether consequent costs are outweighed by purported benefits or not. Openness is not a quality generally associated with the work of security agencies, but without it public debate about the necessity and defensibility of new measures is scarcely possible.

It follows that the principles of *transparency* and *accountability*, though by no means unique to criminal justice, provide a model worthy of emulation in respect of security. To require that security measures have a firm basis in law, be clearly and precisely articulated, be demonstrably necessary, targeted, and, in the case of exceptionally intrusive measures, temporary provides a pragmatic basis for democratic accountability that might delimit their tendency to erode civil liberties. To be effective this must be coupled with adequate provisions to ensure accountability through independent scrutiny of legislation and continuing external oversight by independent actors or review bodies.

Likewise, the criminal justice principle of *proportionality* might provide a way of tying the means more closely to legitimate aims pursued. The requirement articulated in respect of punishment that there be proportionality between the gravity of the offence and the severity of the penalty imposed is a useful model. The conceptual framework of proportionality developed by desert theorists is sophisticated and permits the generation of scales by which to determine the just measure of pain (von Hirsch and Ashworth 2005). The claim to do justice through punishment is, of course, controversial and Shearing has argued that 'logic and morality of retribution that pervades criminal justice . . . should be abandoned' (Shearing 2001b: 206). But abandoning the backward-looking logic of retribution for a future-focused logic of prevention need not entail abandoning the principles carefully articulated by desert theorists to constrain state reaction to crime (Wood 2002). The enquiry whether a response is proportional to the harm done might profitably become a future-oriented enquiry – is this precaution proportional to the risk posed? In respect of the future harms against which security measures are typically deployed, the calculus is a little more complicated. The proportionality of a security measure needs to be tied to the gravity of the prospective harm and then discounted by the likelihood, or not, of it actually occurring (Slobogin 2003). This two-step enquiry furnishes a potential basis for identifying security measures that are disproportional whether to the claimed risks or to their purported goals.

Given the undoubted difficulty of making this two-step calculation in respect of future risks, a further limiting step would be to invoke a principle akin to the presumption of innocence or perhaps a *presumption against threat*. This would have the effect of protecting the interests of those whose liberties would otherwise be compromised by measures justified by poorly founded predictions of harm (Ashworth 2006). Implementing a principle of presumption against threat would make clear that it is not sufficient to belong to a category or class – one must be shown actually to be threatening. But it would also recognize that even the most threatening individual cannot be ascribed culpability before the event, since to do so would be to deny them a window of opportunity in which to choose to do right and, as such, constitute a failure to recognize their moral autonomy.

Although it is hardly possible to import the criminal law principle of certainty in respect of harms yet to occur, a principle of *adequate proof* or a 'firm evidence' requirement should also be introduced. The level at which this is set might vary according to the nature of the measure and the legal channel in which it is pursued, but where the measure is clearly penal in its effect, then the criminal standard of proof beyond all reasonable doubt is appropriate. As a more general matter of security policy, and given the limited confidence that can be placed in most predictions of future harm, at the very least we might posit this requirement negatively, that is to say that uncertainty should not be permitted to license undue intrusions in the name of security (Zedner 2008b).

More generally, security policies should be judged according to principles of *fairness* (that is, they should not burden sub-groups or individuals unduly) and of *equality* (that they should treat all subjects the same irrespective of their age, sex, race, or religion). The distinction between *equality before the law* and the sometimes countervailing principle of *equal impact*, which recognizes that the same restrictions may impose differing burden on different individuals, is also worthy of attention (Ashworth 2000: 79–83). For example the powers of private security guards to exclude people from mass private property on grounds of dress, age, or appearance would be unlikely to satisfy these principles. Generalized suspicion or belonging to a suspect religious, ethnic, or other categorical group would not be sufficient grounds to subject anyone to a burdensome security measure. And in the light of our earlier argument about the need for security measures to conduce to the ends sought, they should also be rights-regarding, and insofar as is possible therefore consistent with such basic civil liberties as freedom of movement, freedom of expression, and individual privacy. The principle of respect for *human rights* and the fostering of a more generalized human rights culture, particularly among the judiciary, are thus essential too. It follows also that security policies should conduce to the basic goods of a flourishing society, not least that they should be productive of trust and social inclusion, and designed to mitigate as far as possible both individual and collective insecurity.

Finally, to ensure powers are used fairly, in accordance with the law and these principles, a robust set of formal complaints procedures, legal challenge through an appeal system, and provision for redress and remedy need to be added to the mix. Collectively, these principles and provisions might be further developed to provide a potentially robust framework for restraining the pursuit of security and, in so doing, defending liberal values.

But it would be a mistake to assume that alone the values and principles of the criminal law, the criminal process, trial, and punishment answer entirely the concerns thrown up by the pursuit of security (Tadros 2007b). The task of governing security requires the development of a new vocabulary and new disciplinary resources with which to describe and to tackle the problems posed. In its prospective orientation, its claim to pre-empt harm and fix the future, security goes beyond the existing remit of criminal law and criminal justice (Ashworth and Zedner 2008, Zedner 2008b) and may require a new normative framework or fresh ethics of security with which to govern its provision. Towards this end an essential first step is the excavation of the entrenched, often hidden assumptions underlying the security agenda to reveal the political and economic interests and intellectual assumptions upon which security policies are based, which it has been the aim of this book to initiate.

Security is constitutive of society in the sense of being a basic ingredient of social interaction and of political community. If security measures are not to damage the flourishing of that community, they need to satisfy public perceptions of legitimacy and of justice. Formulating the basic principles for a 'just security' along the lines suggested above is the surest means to curb the untrammelled urge to seek security by combating crime, terrorism, and other threats with measures that are inconsistent with the requirements of a liberal democratic polity. The human need for security should not be permitted to defeat itself.

NOTES

INTRODUCTION

1 For example, Johnston and Shearing (2003); Valverde (2001: 83–92); Wakefield (2003); Crawford (2002); Hope and Sparks (2000); Loader and Walker (2007); Wood and Shearing (2007).

CHAPTER 1

1 Cited in Mueller (2005: 222–3); with thanks to Marie-Helen Maras for drawing this to my attention. See also H. Boutellier, *The safety utopia: Contemporary discontent and desire as to crime and punishment* (Berlin: Springer, 2004).
2 www.telegraph.co.uk/news/uknews/1422243/Blair-sent-in-tanks-after-'chilling'-threat.html (last accessed 08/12/08).
3 'Tennessee teachers stage fake gunman attack' (14 May 2007) MSNBC, http://www.msnbc.msn.com/id/18645623/ (last accessed 08/12/08).

CHAPTER 2

1 W. Blackstone, *Commentaries on the laws of England*, cited in Radzinowicz (1956: 418).
2 It is noteworthy that in 1978 Foucault declared that if he were able to go

back and correct the theme and title of that year's lectures, he would no longer use the advertised title 'territoire, population, securité' but instead 'lectures on "governmentality" '. But for this fact 'governmentality' scholars would today be 'security' scholars. I am grateful to Mariana Valverde for alerting me to this intriguing fact.

3 In Britain welfare provision built upon existing provision by friendly societies and the cooperative movement and, as such, the origins of the welfare state came as much from below as above.

4 Between 1950 and 1990 the US increased its defence resources from 400 strategic nuclear warheads to over 12,000 and from 462 missile launchers and bombers to 1,900. The Soviet Union increased resources from 84 nuclear warheads in 1956 to over 10,000 and from 22 long-range systems to 2,500 in 1990. Kolodziej (2005: 85–7).

5 By way of example it is estimated that 800,000 people were killed and half a million women were raped in Rwanda in the 1994 genocide. Hoyle and Zedner (2007: 467, 469).

6 UN Secretary-General, Boutros Boutros-Ghali in 1995, quoted in Neocleous (2000a: 7).

7 UN Commission on Human Security (2003), *Human security now*, New York: United Nations. Available online at http://www.humansecurity-chs.org/finalreport/ (last accessed 08/12/08).

CHAPTER 3

1 In Britain this had led to plans to introduce a Points Based System designed to 'build on a package of measures already being introduced to deliver a more secure border'. These include: new electronic checks to count people in and out of the UK, a 'clamp down on illegal immigration'; fingerprinting of visa applicants abroad; and the introduction of ID cards for foreign nationals. The first roll-out of the ID card will also include key security workers, such as airport security guards. Available online at http://www.bia.homeoffice.gov.uk/sitecontent/newsarticles/2007/planstomanagemigration (last accessed 08/12/08).

2 For a fictionalized futuristic account of the ultimate security bubble, see Atwood (2003).

CHAPTER 4

1 For example, Ericson and Haggerty (1997); Jones and Newburn (1998); Garland (2001); Johnston and Shearing (2003); Wakefield (2003); Aas (2007); Ericson (2007); Wood and Shearing (2007).

2 E. Janus, 'The preventive state, terrorists and sexual predators: Countering the threat of a new outsider jurisprudence', *William Mitchell Legal Research Studies Paper* 11 (May 2005): 2. Available at http://ssrn.com/abstract=687165 (date last accessed 08/12/08).

3 Slobogin (2003); Slobogin, 'The civilization of the criminal law', *Vanderbilt Law Review*, 58 (2005): 121–68; E. Janus, 'Civil commitment as social control', in D. Brown and J. Pratt (eds), *Dangerous offenders: Punishment and social order* (London, Routledge, 2000); Janus, 'Hendricks and the moral terrain of police power civil commitment', *Psychology, Public Policy, and Law*, 4 (1998): 297–322; Morse (1998).

4 Investigative journalist David Rose writes: 'Discretionary and automatic life sentences used to be given about 200 times each year. Since coming into force in April 2005, the IPP has been imposed more than 2,000 times, with a rate of over 100 new IPPs each month. As an official told me, Home Office models predict that by 2011, there will be 12,500 inmates serving IPPs – more than three times as many as those doing life for murder.' D. Rose, 'Locked up to make us feel better', *New Statesman* (19 March 2007).

CHAPTER 5

1 On the Marxist reading of security as 'commodity fetishism', see further, Neocleous (2007b).

2 Such research is the subject of a Leverhulme Trust-funded project led by Ian Loader and Benjamin Goold, 'Shopping for security: The meaning and effects of security consumption'.

3 http://www.bsia.co.uk/ (date last accessed 08/12/08).

4 http://www.usatoday.com/money/industries/2006–09–10–security-industry_x.htm (date last accessed 08/12/08).

5 http://www.asial.com.au/default.asp?page=/consumer%20 information/security+industry+overview (date last accessed 08/12/08).

6 http://www.allbusiness.com/specialty-businesses/539469–1.html (date last accessed 08/12/08).

7 http://www.g4s.com/home/ (date last accessed 08/12/08).

8 http://www.securitas.com/en/About-Securitas/ (date last accessed 08/12/08).

9 For example, Group 4 Securicor has acquired both the ArmorGroup, a private military company providing PMC services in Iraq, and Touchcom, a US-based company that develops, installs, and maintains large-scale web-based electronic security systems. It provides security services to the Home Office and the Bank of England, pre-deployment training to the armed forces, protection to US defence facilities, to German army facilities, to the European Parliament, to NATO buildings, and to the Kazakhstan pipeline. http://www.g4s.com/home/our_services/government_expertise.htm (date last accessed 08/12/08).

10 On the limits and inconsistent findings of such research as there is on the private security industry, see Wakefield (2003: ch. 4). See also Johnston (2006); and Abrahamsen and Williams (2007).

11 An anti-theft device, SmartWater[RM] is the registered trade name of a liquid containing a unique DNA-style code which cannot be washed off, lasts for months, and which shows up under ultra-violet light. www.smartwater.com/ (date last accessed 08/12/08).

12 For a different view, see Vindevogel (2005).

13 Home Affairs Committee (1995: ix). See also SIA Annual Report 2003/4: 'The Chairman's View', p.6. http://www.the-sia.org.uk/ (date last accessed 08/12/08).

14 See 'Panoramic Overview of the Private Security Industry in the 25 Member States of the European Union', available online at www.coess.org/stats.htm (date last accessed 08/12/08).

CHAPTER 6

1 In Britain these include the Terrorism Act 2000, the Anti-Terrorism Crime and Security Act 2001, the Prevention of Terrorism Act 2005, the Terrorism Act 2006 and the Counter-Terrorism Bill 2007.

2 After the London bombings, Prime Minister Blair announced a 12-point package of extensive powers that substantially undermine adherence to the European Convention on Human Rights, claiming by way of justification that 'Let no one be in any doubt. The rules of the game are changing . . . for obvious reasons, the mood now is different.' Shami Chakrabarti, 'The Price of a Chilling and Counterproductive Recipe', *The Guardian* (8 August 2005).

3 An excellent analysis of these offences is provided in Tadros (2007b).

4 The so-called 'Belmarsh case', *A* v *SSHD* [2004] UKHL 56; [2005] 2 WLR 87.

5 See the Home Office website: http://security.homeoffice.gov.uk/counter-terrorism-strategy/legislation/pta/ (date last accessed 08/12/08).

6 Special advocates are security-cleared lawyers who are permitted to see sensitive intelligence material but not share or discuss it with their clients.

7 J. Adams, 'What kills you matters, not numbers', *The Social Affairs Unit* (2005), p. 1, available online at http://www.socialaffairsunit.org.uk/blog/archives/000512.php (date last accessed 08/12/08). My thanks to Marie-Helen Maras for drawing this to my attention.

CHAPTER 7

1 For sophisticated treatment of the nature of the right to security and its relationship with other rights, see Fredman (2007); Lazarus (2007).

2 These are rehearsed only briefly here – for a fuller elaboration, see Zedner (2003b: 157).

3 One such model is that of the 'Policing Board', proposed by the 'Patten Commission' on policing in Northern Ireland, whose role is to oversee both police and 'the contributions that people and organisations other than the police can make towards public safety', Northern Ireland Office (1999).

BIBLIOGRAPHY

Aas, K. F. (2004) 'From narrative to database: Technological change and penal culture', *Punishment and Society*, 6(4): 379–93.

Aas, K. F. (2007) *Globalization and crime*, London: Sage.

Aas, K. F., Oppen Gundhus, H. and Mork Lomell, H. (eds) (2008) *Technologies of insecurity: The surveillance of everyday life*, London: Routledge.

Aas, K. F. (forthcoming) ' "Security-at-a-distance": Globalization and the shifting boundaries of criminology', in I. Loader and S. Percy (eds), *The new economy of security: Contemporary insecurities and the pluralization of coercive force*, Cambridge: Cambridge University Press.

Abrahamsen, R. and Williams, M. C. (eds) (2007) 'The privatisation and globalisation of security in Africa', *International Relations*, Special Issue, 21/2: 131–41.

Ackerman, B. (2004) 'The emergency constitution', *Yale Law Journal*, 113(5): 1029–91.

Agamben, G. (2004) *The state of exception*, Chicago: University of Chicago Press.

Albrecht, H. (1997) 'Ethnic minorities, crime, and criminal justice in Germany', *Crime and Justice: A Review of Research*, 21: 31–99.

Albrecht, H. (2000) 'Foreigners, migration, immigration and the development of criminal justice in Europe', in P. Green and A. Rutherford (eds), *Criminal policy in transition*, Oxford: Hart Publishing.

Aradau, C. and van Munster, R. (2007) 'Governing terrorism through risk: Taking precautions, (un)knowing the future', *European Journal of International Relations*, 13: 89–115.

Ashworth, A. (2000) *Sentencing and criminal justice*, London: Butterworths.

Ashworth, A. (2002) *Human rights, serious crime and criminal procedure*, London: Sweet & Maxwell.

Ashworth, A. (2004) 'Social control and "anti-social behaviour": The subversion of human rights?', *Law Quarterly Review*, 120: 263–91.

Ashworth, A. (2006) 'Four threats to the presumption of innocence', *South African Law Journal*, 123: 62–96.

Ashworth, A. (2007) 'Security, terrorism and the value of human rights', in B. Goold and L. Lazarus (eds), *Security and human rights*, Oxford: Hart Publishing, pp. 203–26.

Ashworth, A. and Zedner, L. (2008) 'Defending the criminal law: Reflections on the changing character of crime, procedure, and sanctions', *Criminal Law and Philosophy*, 2: 21–51.

Atwood, M. (2003) *Oryx and crake*, London: Virago.

Avant, D. (2005) *The market for force: The consequences of privatizing security*, Cambridge: Cambridge University Press.

Bauman, Z. (1998) *Globalization: The human consequences*, Cambridge: Polity.

Bayley, D. and C. Shearing (1996) 'The future of policing', *Law and Society Review*, 30(3): 585–606.

Bentham, J. (1843) *The works of Jeremy Bentham, Principles of the civil code*, Edinburgh: William Tait.

Berki, R. N. (1986) *Security and society: Reflections on law, order and politics*, London: J. M. Dent & Sons.

Bernstein, P. (1998) *Against the gods: The remarkable story of risk*, New York: Wiley.

Bigo, D. (2000) 'Liaison officers in Europe: New officers in the European security field', in J. Sheptycki (ed.), *Issues in transnational policing*, London: Routledge, pp. 67–99.

Bigo, D. (2001) 'The mobius ribbon of internal and external security', in M. Albert, D. Jacobson and Y. Lapid (eds), *Identities, borders, orders: Rethinking international relations theory*, Minneapolis: University of Minnesota Press, pp. 91–115.

Bigo, D. (2006) 'Internal and external aspects of security', *European Security*, 15(4): 385–404.

Blakely, E. and Snyder, M. (1997) *Fortress America: Gated communities in the United States*, Washington, DC: Brookings Institution Press.

Bonner, D. (2006) 'Checking the executive? Detention without trial, control orders, due process and human rights', *European Public Law*, 12(1): 45–71.

Booth, K. (1991) 'Security and emancipation,' *Review of International Studies*, 17(4): 313–26.

Bosworth, M. (2008) 'Border control and the limits of the sovereign state', *Social and Legal Studies*, 17(2): 199–215.

Bothe, M. (2003) 'Terrorism and the legality of pre-emptive force', *European Journal of International Law*, 14(2): 227–40.

Bottoms, A. E. and Brownsword, R. (1982) 'The dangerousness debate after the Floud Report', *British Journal of Criminology*, 22: 229–54.

Boutellier, H. (2004) *The safety utopia: Contemporary discontent and desire as to crime and punishment*, Berlin: Springer.

Braithwaite, J. (2000) 'The new regulatory state and the transformation of criminology', in D. Garland and R. Sparks (eds), *Criminology and social theory*, Oxford: Oxford University Press, pp. 47–69.

Braithwaite, J. (2006) 'Pre-empting terrorism', *Current Issues in Criminal Justice*, 17(1): 96–114.

Braithwaite, J. and Levi-Faur, D. (2008) *Regulatory capitalism: How it works, ideas for making it work better*, Cheltenham: Edward Elgar.

Brodeur, J.-P. and Shearing, C. (2005) 'Configuring security and justice', *European Journal of Criminology*, 2(4): 379–406.

Buchanan, J. M. (1965) 'An economic theory of clubs', *Economica*, 32(125): 1–14.

Burchell, G. (1991) 'Peculiar interests: Civil society and governing "The System of Natural Liberty" ', in G. Burchell, C. Gordon and P. Miller (eds), *The Foucault effect: Studies in governmentality*, Hemel Hempstead: Harvester Wheatsheaf, pp. 119–50.

Burchell, G., Gordon, C. and Miller, P. (eds) (1991) *The Foucault effect: Studies in governmentality*, Hemel Hempstead: Harvester Wheatsheaf.

Burney, E. (2005) *Making people behave: Anti-social behaviour, politics and policy*, Cullompton: Willan Publishing.

Button, M. (2003) 'Private security and the policing of quasi-public space', *International Journal of the Sociology of Law*, 31: 227–37.

Buzan, B. (1991) *People, states and fear*, London: Harvester Wheatsheaf.

Buzan, B., Waever, O. and de Wilde, J. (1998) *Security: A new framework for analysis*, London: Lynne Rienner.

Cabinet Office (2007) *Security in a global hub: Establishing the UK's new border arrangements*, London: HMSO.

Cavadino, M. and Dignan, J. (2006) *Penal systems: A comparative approach*, London: Sage.

Chadwick, E. (1829) 'Preventive police', *London Review*, 1: 252–308.

Chesterman, S. and Lehnhardt, C. (2007) *From mercenaries to market: The rise and regulation of private military companies*, Oxford: Oxford University Press.

Christie, N. (1994) *Crime control as industry*, London: Routledge.

Clarke, R. V. (1995) 'Situational crime prevention', in M. Tonry and N. Morris (eds), *Crime and justice: An annual review of research*, Chicago: University of Chicago, 19: 91–150.

Coase, R. (1974) 'The lighthouse in economics', *Journal of Law and Economics*, 17(2): 357–76.

Cohen, S. (1980) *Folk devils and moral panics*, Oxford: Martin Robertson.

Cole, D. (2003) *Enemy aliens: Double standards and constitutional freedoms in the war on terrorism*, New York: The New Press.

Cole, D. (2004) 'The priority of morality: The emergency constitution's blind spot', *Yale Law Journal*, 113(8): 1753–800.

Crawford, A. (1998) 'Community safety and the quest for security: Holding back the dynamics of social exclusion', *Policy Studies*, 19(374): 237–53.

Crawford, A. (ed.) (2002) *Crime and insecurity: The governance of safety in Europe*, Cullompton: Willan Publishing.

Crawford, A. (2003) ' "Contractual governance" of deviant behaviour', *Journal of Law and Society*, 30(4): 479–505.

Crawford, A. (2006a) 'Networked governance and the post-regulatory state? Steering, rowing and anchoring the provision of policing and security', *Theoretical Criminology*, 10(4): 449–79.

Crawford, A. (2006b) 'Policing and security as "club goods": The new enclosures?', in J. Wood and B. Dupont (eds), *Democracy and the governance of security*, Cambridge: Cambridge University Press, pp. 111–38.

Crawford, A. and Lister, S. (2004) 'The patchwork shape of reassurance policing in England and Wales: Integrated local security quilts, or frayed, fragmented and fragile tangled webs?', *Policing*, 27(3): 413–30.

Crawford, A., Lister, S., Blackburn, S. and Burnett, J. (2005) *Plural policing: The mixed economy of visible patrols*, Bristol: The Policy Press.

Currie, E. (1997) 'Market, crime and community: Towards a mid-range theory of post-industrial violence', *Theoretical Criminology*, 1(2): 147–72.

Dauvergne, C. (2007) 'Security and migration law in a less brave new world', *Social and Legal Studies*, 16(4): 533–49.

Davis, M. (1990) *City of quartz: Excavating the future in Los Angeles*, London: Pimlico.

De Lint, W. and Virta, S. (2004) 'Security in ambiguity: Towards a radical security politics', *Theoretical Criminology*, 8(4): 465–89.

Deflem, M. (ed.) (2004) *Terrorism and counter-terrorism: Criminological perspectives*, Amsterdam: Elsevier.

Dershowitz, A. (2006) *Preemption: A knife that cuts both ways*, New York: W. W. Norton.

Dinh, V. (2002) 'Freedom and security after September 11', *Harvard Journal of Law and Public Policy*, 25: 399–406.

Dinwiddy, J. (1978) 'The classical economists and the utilitarians', in E. K. Bramsted and K. J. Melhuish (eds), *Western liberalism: A history in documents from Locke to Croce*, London: Longman, pp. 12–25.

Dixon, D. (1997) *Law in policing: Legal regulation and police practices*, Oxford: Clarendon Press.

Dorn, N. and Levi, M. (2007) 'European private security, corporate investigation and military services: Collective security, market regulation and structuring the public sphere', *Policing & Society*, 17(3): 213–38.

Dubber, M. D. (2005) *The police power: Patriarchy and the foundations of American government*, New York: Columbia University Press.

Dubber, M. D. and Valverde, M. (eds) (2006) *The new police science: The police power in domestic and international law*, Stanford: Stanford University Press.

Duff, R. A. (1986) *Trials and punishments*, Cambridge: Cambridge University Press.

Duff, R. A. and Garland, D. (eds) (1994) *A reader on punishment*, Oxford: Oxford University Press.

Duff, R. A. and Marshall, S. (2000) 'Benefits, burdens and responsibilities: Some ethical dimensions of situational crime prevention', in A. von Hirsch, D. Garland and A. Wakefield (eds), *Ethical and social perspectives on situational crime prevention*, Oxford: Hart Publishing, pp. 17–35.

Dupont, B. (2004) 'Security through networks: Surveying the relational landscape of security managers in an urban setting', *Crime, Law and Social Change*, 45: 165–84.

Dupont, B. (2006) 'Delivering security in the age of networks', *Policing & Society*, 14(1, March): 76–91.

Dupont, B., Grabosky, P. N. and Shearing, C. (2003) 'The governance of security in weak and failing states', *Criminal Justice* 3(4): 331–49.

Dupont, B. and Wood, J. (eds) (2006) *Democracy, society and the governance of security*, Cambridge: Cambridge University Press.

Dworkin, R. (2002) 'The threat to patriotism', *New York Review of Books*, 49(3), available online at http://www.nybooks.com/articles/15145 (date last accessed 08/12/08).

Dworkin, R. (2003) 'Terror and the attack on civil liberties', *New York Review of Books*, 50(17), available online at http://www.nybooks.com/articles/article-preview?article_id=16738 (date last accessed 08/12/08).

Dyzenhaus, D. (2001) 'The permanence of the temporary: Can emergency powers be normalized?', in R. Daniels, P. Macklem and K. Roach (eds), *The security of freedom: Essays on Canada's anti-terrorism bill*, Toronto: Toronto University Press, pp. 21–37.

Dyzenhaus, D. (2007) 'Deference, security, and human rights', in L. Lazarus and B. J. Goold (eds), *Security and human rights*, Oxford: Hart Publishing.

Eide, E. (2000) 'Economics of criminal behaviour', in B. Bouckaert and G. de Geest (eds), *Encyclopedia of law and economics*, Ghent: Edward Elgar, pp. 345–89.

Ellison, G. and O'Reilly, C. (2008) 'Ulster's policing goes global': The police reform process in Northern Ireland and the creation of a global brand,' *Crime Law and Social Change*, 50(4): 331–51.

Ericson, R. (1994) 'The division of expert knowledge in policing and security', *British Journal of Sociology*, 45(2): 149–75.

Ericson, R. (2007) *Crime in an insecure world*, Cambridge: Polity.

Ericson, R., Barry, D. and Doyle, A. (2000) 'The moral hazards of neoliberalism: Lessons from the private insurance industry', *Economy and Society* 29(4): 532–58.

Ericson, R. and Doyle, A. (2004) *Uncertain business: Risk, insurance and the limits of knowledge*, Toronto: University of Toronto Press.

Ericson, R., Doyle, A. and Barry, D. (2003) *Insurance as governance*, Toronto: University of Toronto Press.

Ericson, R. and Haggerty, K. (1997) *Policing the risk society*, Oxford: Oxford University Press.

Farmer, L. (2006) 'The jurisprudence of security: The police power and the criminal law', in M. D. Dubber and M. Valverde (eds), *The new police science: The police power in domestic and international perspective*, Stanford: Stanford University Press.

Feeley, M. (2002) 'Entrepreneurs of punishment: The legacy of privatization', *Punishment and Society*, 4(3): 321–44.

Feeley, M. (2004) 'Actuarial justice and the modern state', in G. Bruinsma, H. Elffers and J. de Keijser (eds), *Punishment, places, and perpetrators: Developments in criminology and criminal justice research*, Cullompton: Willan Publishing, pp. 62–77.

Feeley, M. and Simon, J. (1992) 'The new penology: Notes on the emerging strategy of corrections and its implications', *Criminology*, 30(4): 449–74.

Feeley, M. and Simon, J. (1994) 'Actuarial justice: The emerging new criminal law', in D. Nelken (ed.), *The futures of criminology*, London: Sage, pp. 173–201.

Feldman, N. (2002) 'Choices of law, choices of war', *Harvard Journal of Law and Public Policy*, 25(2): 457–85.

Felson, M. (2002) *Crime and everyday life*, London: Sage.

Felson, M. and Clarke, R. V. (1998) *Opportunity makes the thief: Practical theory for crime prevention*. Police Research Series No. 98, London: Home Office.

Fenwick, H. (2002) 'The Anti-Terrorism, Crime and Security Act 2001: A proportionate response to 11 September?', *Modern Law Review*, 65(5): 724–62.

Fisher, E. (2005) 'Risk and environmental law: A beginner's guide', in B. Richardson and S. Wood (eds), *Environmental law for sustainability: A critical reader*, Oxford: Hart Publishing.

Floud, J. and Young, W. (1981) *Dangerousness and criminal justice*, London: Heinemann.

Foucault, M. (1979) *Discipline and punish: The birth of the prison*, Harmondsworth, Middlesex: Peregrine.

Foucault, M. (1991) 'Governmentality', in G. Burchell, C. Gordon and P. Miller (eds), *The Foucault effect*, London: Harvester Wheatsheaf, pp. 87–104.

Foucault, M. (2007) *Security, territory, population* (trans. ed.), London: Palgrave Macmillan.

Fredman, S. (2007) 'The positive right to security', in B. Goold and L. Lazarus (eds), *Security and human rights*, Oxford: Hart Publishing, pp. 307–24.

Freedman, L. (1998) 'International security: Changing targets', *Foreign Policy*, 110: 48–63.

Freedman, L. (2003) 'The concept of security', in M. Hawkesworth (ed.), *Encyclopedia of government and politics*, London: Routledge.

Freedman, L. (2004) *Deterrence*, Cambridge: Polity Press.

Friedrichs, J. (2008) *Fighting terrorism and drugs: European and international police cooperation*, London: Routledge.

Gambetta, D. (1993) *The Sicilian Mafia: The business of private protection*, Cambridge, MA: Harvard University Press.

Gardiner, S. M. (2006) 'A core precautionary principle', *Journal of Political Philosophy*, 14(1): 33–60.

Garland, D. (1985) *Punishment and welfare: A history of penal strategies*, London: Gower.

Garland, D. (2001) *The culture of control: Crime and social order in contemporary society*, Oxford: Oxford University Press.

Gill, M. and Hart, J. (1999) 'Enforcing corporate security policy using private investigators', *European Journal on Criminal Policy and Research*, 7: 245–61.

Gill, P. (2003) 'Security and intelligence systems in the United Kingdom', in J.-P. Brodeur, P. Gill and D. Töllborg (eds), *Democracy, law and security: Internal security services in contemporary Europe*, Aldershot: Ashgate, pp. 265–93.

Golove, D. and Holmes, S. (2004) 'Terrorism and accountability: Why checks and balances apply even in "The War on Terrorism" ', *NYU Review of Law and Security*, 2: 2–7.

Goold, B. (2007) 'Privacy, identity and security', in B. Goold and L. Lazarus (eds), *Security and human rights*, Oxford: Hart Publishing, pp. 45–71.

Goold, B. (2009) *Surveillance*, London: Routledge.

Goold, B. and Lazarus, L. (eds) (2007) *Security and human rights*, Oxford: Hart Publishing.

Goold, B. (2004) *CCTV and policing: Public area surveillance and police practices in Britain*, Oxford: Oxford University Press.

Gross, O. (2001) 'Cutting down trees: Law-making under the shadow of great calamities', in R. Daniels, P. Macklem and K. Roach (eds), *The security of freedom: Essays on Canada's anti-terrorism bill*, Toronto: Toronto University Press, pp. 39–61.

Gross, O. (2003) 'Chaos and rules: Should responses to violent crises always be constitutional?', *Yale Law Journal*, 112(5): 1011–134.

Günther, K. (2005) 'World citizens between freedom and security', *Constellations*, 12(3): 379–91.

Hacking, I. (1986) 'Making up people', in T. Heller (ed.), *Reconstructing individualism*, Stanford: Stanford University Press, pp. 222–36.

Hacking, I. (1990) *The taming of chance*, Cambridge: Cambridge University Press.

Hadfield, P. (2006) *Bar wars: Contesting the night in contemporary British cities*, Oxford: Oxford University Press.

Haggerty, K. (2003) 'From risk to precaution: The rationalities of personal crime prevention', in R. Ericson and A. Doyle (eds), *Risk and morality*, Toronto: University of Toronto Press, pp. 193–214.

Harcourt, B. (2007) *Against prediction: Profiling, policing, and punishing in an actuarial age*, Chicago: University of Chicago Press.

Hayek, F. A. (1960) *The constitution of liberty*, Chicago: Chicago University Press.

Heymann, P. (2002) 'Civil liberties and human rights in the aftermath of September 11', *Harvard Journal of Law and Public Policy*, 25: 441–56.

Hill, P. (2003) *The Japanese Mafia: Yakuza, law, and the state*, Oxford: Oxford University Press.

Hillyard, P. (1994) 'The normalization of special powers from Northern Ireland to Britain', in N. Lacey (ed.), *A reader on criminal justice*, Oxford: Oxford University Press, pp. 63–102.

Hindess, B. (1993) 'Rational choice theory', in W. Outhwaite and T. Bottomore (eds), *The Blackwell dictionary of twentieth-century social thought*, Oxford: Blackwell Publishers, pp. 542–3.

Hobbes, T. (1651) *Leviathan*, London: Penguin Classics.

Hobbs, D., Hadfield, P., Lister, S. and Winlow, S. (2002) ' "Door Lore": The art and economics of intimidation', *British Journal of Criminology*, 42(2): 352–70.

Hobbs, D., Hadfield, P., Lister, S. and Winlow, S. (2003) *Bouncers: Violence and governance in the night time economy*, Oxford: Oxford University Press.

Home Affairs Committee (1995) *First report on the private security industry*, London: HMSO.

Hood, C. (1998) *The art of the state: Culture, rhetoric, and public management*, Oxford: Oxford University Press.

Hood, R., Shute, S., Feilzer, M. and Wilcox, A. (2002) 'Sex offenders emerging from long-term imprisonment: A study of their long-term reconviction rates and of parole board members' judgements of their risk', *British Journal of Criminology*, 42: 371–94.

Hoogenboom, A. B. (1991) 'Grey policing: A theoretical framework', *Policing and Society*, 2(1): 17–30.

Hope, T. (2000) 'Inequality and the clubbing of private security', in T. Hope and R. Sparks (eds), *Crime, risk and insecurity*, London: Routledge, pp. 83–106.

Hope, T. and Sparks, R. (eds) (2000) *Crime, risk and insecurity: Law and order in everyday life and political discourse*, London: Routledge.

Hoyle, C. (2008) 'Will she be safe? A critical analysis of risk assessment in domestic violence cases', *Children and Youth Services Review*, 30(3): 323–37.

Hoyle, C. and Zedner, L. (2007) 'Victims, victimization and criminal justice', in M. Maguire, R. Morgan and R. Reiner (eds), *The Oxford handbook of criminology*, Oxford: Oxford University Press, pp. 461–95.

Hudson, B. (2003) *Justice in the risk society*, London: Sage.

Huey, L., Ericson, R. and Haggerty, K. (2005) 'Policing fantasy city', in D. Cooley (ed.), *Re-imagining policing in Canada*, Toronto: University of Toronto Press, pp. 140–208.

Hughes, G. (1998) *Understanding crime prevention: Social control, risk and late modernity*, Buckingham: Open University Press.

Huysmans, J. (2006) *The politics of insecurity: Fear, migration and asylum in the EU*, London: Routledge.

Ignatieff, M. (1978) *A just measure of pain: The penitentiary in the industrial revolution 1750–1850*, London: Macmillan.

Ignatieff, M. (2004) *The lesser evil: Political ethics in an age of terror*, Edinburgh: Edinburgh University Press.

Innes, M. (2004) 'Reinventing tradition? Reassurance, neighbourhood security and policing', *Criminal Justice*, 4(2): 151–71.

Janus, E. (1998) 'Hendricks and the moral terrain of police power civil commitment', *Psychology, Public Policy, and Law*, 4: 297–322.

Janus, E. (2000) 'Civil commitment as social control', in D. Brown and J. Pratt (eds), *Dangerous offenders: Punishment and social order*, London: Routledge, pp. 71–90.

Janus, E. (2005) 'The preventive state, terrorists and sexual predators: Countering the threat of a new outsider jurisprudence', available at http://ssrn.com/abstract=687165 (date last accessed 08/12/08), pp. 17–30.

Johnston, L. (1992) *The rebirth of private policing*, London: Routledge.

Johnston, L. (1996) 'What is vigilantism?', *British Journal of Criminology*, 36: 220–36.

Johnston, L. (1999a) *Policing Britain: Risk, security and governance*, Harlow: Longman.

Johnston, L. (1999b) 'Private policing in context', *European Journal on Criminal Policy and Research*, 7(2): 175–96.

Johnston, L. (2003) 'From "pluralisation" to "the police extended family": Discourses on the governance of community policing in Britain', *International Journal of the Sociology of Law*, 31: 185–204.

Johnston, L. (2006) 'Transnational security governance', in J. Wood and D. Dupont (eds), *Democracy, society and the governance of security*, Cambridge: Cambridge University Press, pp. 33–51.

Johnston, L. and Shearing, C. (2003) *Governing security: Explorations in policing and justice*, London: Routledge.

Jones, R. (2005) 'Surveillance', in C. Hale, K. Hayward, A. Wahidin and E. Wincup (eds), *Criminology*, Oxford: Oxford University Press, pp. 471–507.

Jones, T. (2007) 'The governance of security', in M. Maguire, R. Morgan and R. Reiner (eds), *The Oxford handbook of criminology*, Oxford: Oxford University Press, pp. 841–65.

Jones, T. and Newburn, T. (1998) *Private security and public policing*, Oxford: Oxford University Press.

Jones, T. and Newburn, T. (1999) 'Urban change and policing: Mass private property re-considered', *European Journal on Criminal Policy and Research*, 7(2): 225–44.

Jones, T. and Newburn, T. (2002) 'The transformation of policing? Understanding current trends in policing systems', *British Journal of Criminology*, 42(1): 129–46.

Jordana, J. and Levi-Faur, D. (eds) (2004) *The politics of regulation: Institutions and regulatory reforms for the governance age*, Cheltenham: Edward Elgar.

Katyal, N. and Tribe, L. (2002) 'Waging war, deciding guilt: Trying the military tribunals', *Yale Law Journal*, 111(6): 1259–310.

Kelly, P. J. (1990) *Utilitarianism and distributive justice*, Oxford: Clarendon Press.

Kemshall, H. and Maguire, M. (2001) 'Public protection, partnership and risk penality: The multi-agency risk management of sexual and violent offenders', *Punishment and Society*, 3(2): 237–64.

King, G. and Murray, C. (2001–2) 'Rethinking human security', *Political Science Quarterly*, 116: 585–610.

Klein, N. (2007) *The shock doctrine: The rise of disaster capitalism*, New York: Metropolitan Books.

Kleinig, J. (2000) 'The burdens of situational crime prevention', in A. von Hirsch, D. Garland and A. Wakefield (eds), *Ethical and social perspectives on situational crime prevention*, Oxford: Hart Publishing, pp. 37–58.

Kneymeyer, F.-L. (1980) 'Polizei', *Economy and Society*, 9(2): 172–96.

Kolodziej, E. A. (2005) *Security and international relations*, Cambridge: Cambridge University Press.

Kostakopoulou, D. (2008) 'How to do things with security post 9/11', *Oxford Journal of Legal Studies*, 28(2): 317–42.

Kraakman, R. (1986) 'Gatekeepers: The anatomy of a third-party enforcement strategy', *Journal of Law, Economics, and Organization*, 2(1): 53–104.

Krahmann, E. (2008) 'Security: Collective good or commodity?', *European Journal of International Relations*, 14(3): 379–404.

Krasmann, S. (2007) 'The enemy on the border: Critique of a programme in favour of a preventive state', *Punishment and Society*, 9(3): 301–18.

Krause, K. and Williams, M. C. (eds) (1997) *Critical security studies: Cases and concepts*, Minneapolis: University of Minnesota Press.

Lacey, N. (2008) *The prisoners' dilemma: Political economy and punishment in contemporary democracies*, Cambridge: Cambridge University Press.

Lazarus, L. (2007) 'Mapping the right to security', in B. Goold and L. Lazarus (eds), *Security and human rights*, Oxford: Hart Publishing, pp. 325–46.

Lepsius, O. (2004) 'Liberty, security, and terrorism: The legal position in Germany', *German Law Journal*, 5(1): 435–60.

Levi-Faur, D. (2005) 'The global diffusion of regulatory capitalism', *Annals of the American Academy of Political and Social Science*, 598: 12–32.

Levi, M. and Wall, D. (2004) 'Technologies, security, and privacy in the post 9/11 European information society', *Journal of Law and Society*, 31(2): 194–220.

Lister, S., Hadfield, P., Hobbs, D. and Winlow, S. (2001) 'Accounting for bouncers: Occupational licensing as a mechanism for regulation', *Criminal Justice*, 1(4): 363–84.

Loader, I. (1997a) 'Private security and the demand for protection in contemporary Britain', *Policing and Society*, 7: 143–62.

Loader, I. (1997b) 'Thinking normatively about private security', *Journal of Law and Society*, 24(5): 377–94.

Loader, I. (1999) 'Consumer culture and the commodification of policing and security', *Sociology*, 33(2): 373–92.

Loader, I. (2000) 'Plural policing and democratic governance', *Social and Legal Studies*, 9(3): 323–45.

Loader, I. (2002) 'Policing, securitization and democracy in Europe', *Criminal Justice*, 2(2): 125–53.

Loader, I. (2006) ' "Fall of the platonic guardians": Liberalism, criminology and political responses in England and Wales', *British Journal of Criminology*, 46(4): 561–86.

Loader, I. (2008) 'The anti-politics of crime', *Theoretical Criminology*, 12(3): 399–410.

Loader, I. and Walker, N. (2001) 'Policing as a public good: Reconstituting the connections between policing and the state', *Theoretical Criminology*, 5(1): 9–35.

Loader, I. and Walker, N. (2004) 'State of denial? Rethinking the governance of security', *Punishment and Society*, 6(2): 221–8.

Loader, I. and Walker, N. (2005) 'Necessary virtues: The legitimate place of the state in the production of security', in B. Dupont and J. Wood (eds), *Democracy, society and the governance of security*, Cambridge: Cambridge University Press.

Loader, I. and Walker, N. (2006) 'Locating the public interest in transnational policing', in A. Goldsmith and J. Sheptycki (eds), *Crafting global policing*, Oxford: Hart Publishing.

Loader, I. and Walker, N. (2007) *Civilizing security*, Cambridge: Cambridge University Press.

Locke, J. (1690) *Two treatises of government*, Cambridge: Cambridge University Press.

Low, S. (2003) *Behind the gates: Life, security and the pursuit of happiness in Fortress America*, New York: Routledge.

Lowe, V. (2005) ' "Clear and present danger": Responses to terrorism', *International and Comparative Law Quarterly*, 54: 185–96.

Lustgarten, L. and Leigh, I. (1994) *In from the cold: National security and parliamentary democracy*, Oxford: Oxford University Press.

Lynch, A. and Reilly, A. (2007) 'The constitutional validity of terrorism orders of control and preventative detention', *Flinders Journal of Law Reform*, 10: 105–42.

Lyon, D. (2001) *Surveillance society: Monitoring everyday life*, Milton Keynes: Open University Press.

Lyon, D. (2007a) 'How did we get here?', *Criminal Justice Matters: Security and Surveillance*, 68: 4–5.

Lyon, D. (2007b) *Surveillance studies: An overview*, Cambridge: Polity Press.

MacFarlane, S. N. and Khong, Y. F. (2006) *Human security and the UN: A critical history*, Bloomington: Indiana University Press.

Maras, M.-H. (2008) 'From targeted to mass surveillance: The consequences and costs of the data retention directive', Oxford: DPhil dissertation.

Marks, M. and Goldsmith, A. (2006) 'The state, the people and democratic policing: The case of South Africa', in J. Wood and B. Dupont (eds), *Democracy, society and the governance of security*, Cambridge: Cambridge University Press, pp. 139–64.

Martinson, R. (1974) 'What works? Questions and answers about prison reform', *Public Interest* (Spring): 22–54.

Marx, G. T. (1995) 'The engineering of social control: The search for the silver bullet', in J. Hagan and R. Peterson (eds), *Crime and inequality*, Stanford: Stanford University Press.

Marx, G. T. (2001) 'Murky conceptual waters: The public and the private', *Ethics and Information Technology*, 3(3): 157–69.

McCulloch, J. and Carlton, B. (2006) 'Preempting justice: Suppression of financing of terrorism and the "War on Terror" ', *Current Issues in Criminal Justice*, 17(3): 397–412.

McMullen, J. (1996) 'The new improved monied police: Reform, crime control, and the commodification of policing in London', *British Journal of Criminology*, 36(1): 85–108.

McMullen, J. (1998) 'The arresting eye: Discourse, surveillance and disciplinary administration in early English police thinking', *Social and Legal Studies* 7(1): 97–128.

McSherry, B. (2008) 'Expanding the boundaries of inchoate crimes: The growing reliance on preparatory offences', in B. McSherry, A. Norrie and S. Bronitt (eds), *Regulating deviance: The redirection of criminalisation and the futures of criminal law*, Oxford: Hart Publishing.

McSweeney, B. (1999) *Security, identity and interests: A sociology of international relations*, Cambridge: Cambridge University Press.

Melossi, D. and Pavarini, M. (1981) *The prison and the factory*, London: Macmillan.

Mill, J. S. (1972) *Utilitarianism: On liberty and considerations of representative government*, London: Dent and Sons.

Mill, J. S. (1979) *On liberty*, Harmondsworth, Middlesex: Penguin.

Monahan, J. (2006) 'A jurisprudence of risk assessment: Forecasting harm among prisoners, predators, and patients', *Virginia Law Review*, 92(3): 391–435.

Moran, M. (2003) *The British regulatory state: High modernism and hyper-innovation*, Oxford: Oxford University Press.

Morse, S. J. (1998) ' Fear of danger, flight from culpability', *Psychology, Public Policy, and Law*, 4: 250–67.

Mueller, J. (2005) 'Simplicity and spook: Terrorism and the dynamics of threat exaggeration', *International Studies Perspectives*, 6: 208–34.

Mythen, G. and Walklate, S. (2008) 'Terrorism, risk and international security: The perils of asking "What if?" ', *Security Dialogue*, 39: 221–42.

Neocleous, M. (2000a) 'Against security', *Radical Philosophy*, 100: 7–15.

Neocleous, M. (2000b) *The fabrication of social order: A critical theory of police power*, London: Pluto Press.

Neocleous, M. (2007a) 'Theoretical foundations of the "new police science" ', in M. D. Dubber and M. Valverde (eds), *The new police science: The police power in domestic and international governance*, Stanford: Stanford University Press, pp. 17–41.

Neocleous, M. (2007b) 'Security, commodity, fetishism', *Critique*, 35(3): 339–55.

Neocleous, M. (2008) *Critique of security*, Edinburgh: Edinburgh University Press.

Newburn, T. (2001) 'The commodification of policing: Security networks in the late modern city', *Urban Studies*, 38(5–6): 829–48.

Newburn, T. (2006) 'Contrasts in intolerance: Cultures of control in the United States and Britain', in T. Newburn and P. Rock (eds), *The politics of crime control*, Oxford: Oxford University Press, pp. 227–70.

Nickel, J. (2007) 'Due process rights and terrorist emergencies', *European Journal of Legal Studies*, 1, available online at http://www.ejls.eu/1/12UK.pdf (date last accessed 08/12/08).

Norris, C. and Armstrong, G. (1999) *The maximum surveillance society: The rise of CCTV*, Oxford: Berg.

Northern Ireland Office (1999) *A new beginning: Policing in Northern Ireland. Report of the Independent Commission on Policing for Northern Ireland (The Patten Report)*, Belfast: Northern Ireland Office.

Nozick, R. (1974) *Anarchy, state and utopia*, Oxford: Blackwell.

Nuotio, K. (2006) 'Terrorism as a catalyst for the emergence, harmonization and reform of criminal law', *Journal of International Criminal Justice*, 4(5): 998–1016.

O'Malley, P. (1992) 'Risk, power, and crime prevention', *Economy and Society*, 21(3): 252–75.

O'Malley, P. (1999) 'Volatile and contradictory punishment', *Theoretical Criminology*, 3: 175–96.

O'Malley, P. (2001) 'Risk, crime and prudentialism revisited', in K. Stenson and R. R. Sullivan (eds), *Crime, risk and justice: The politics of crime control in liberal democracies*, Cullompton: Willan Publishing, pp. 89–103.

O'Malley, P. (2004a) *Risk, uncertainty and government*, London: The Glass-house Press.

O'Malley, P. (2004b) 'The uncertain promise of risk', *Australian and New Zealand Journal of Criminology*, 37(3): 323–43.

O'Reilly, C. (forthcoming) *Policing global risks: The transnational security consultancy industry*, Oxford: Hart Publishing.

O'Reilly, C. and Ellison, G. (2006) 'Eye spy private high: Re-conceptualizing high policing theory', *British Journal of Criminology*, 46: 641–60.

Ocqueteau, F. (1993) 'Legitimation of the private security sector in France', *European Journal on Criminal Policy and Research*, 1(4): 108–22.

Ogata, S. (2003) 'A new concept of human security', *International Herald Tribune*, 8 May.

Osborne, D. and Gaebler, T. (1992) *Reinventing government: How the entrepreneurial spirit is transforming the public sector*, New York: Penguin.

Packer, H. L. (1968) *The limits of the criminal sanction*, Stanford: Stanford University Press.

Paris, R. (2001) 'Human security: Paradigm shift or hot air?', *International Security*, 26(2): 87–102.

Patane, V. (2006) 'Recent Italian efforts to respond to terrorism at the legislative level', *Journal of International Criminal Justice*, 4(5): 1166–80.

Pavarini, M. (1997) 'Controlling social panic: Questions and answers about security in Italy at the end of the millennium', in R. Bergalli and C. Sumner (eds), *Social control and political order: European perspectives at the end of the century*, London: Sage, pp. 75–95.

Percy, S. (2007) *Mercenaries: The history of a norm in international relations*, Oxford: Oxford University Press.

Posner, R. (2006) *Not a suicide pact: The constitution in a time of national emergency*, New York: Oxford University Press.

Power, M. (2004) *The risk management of everything*, London: Demos.

Pratt, J. (2007) *Penal populism*, London: Routledge.

Pratt, J., Brown, D., Brown, M., Hallsworth, S. and Morrison, W. (eds) (2005) *The new punitiveness: Trends, theories, perspectives*, Cullompton: Willan Publishing.

Prenzler, T. and Sarre, R. (1998) 'Regulating private security in Australia', *Australian Institute of Criminology: Trends and Issues in Crime and Criminal Justice*, 98: 1–6.

Radzinowicz, L. (1956) *A history of English criminal law and its administration from 1750*, vol. 3, London: Steven & Sons Limited.

Radzinowicz, L. and Hood, R. (1981) 'Dangerousness and criminal justice', *Criminal Law Review*, 756–61.

Ramsay, P. (2004) 'What is anti-social behaviour?', *Criminal Law Review*, 908–25.

Rawls, J. (1973) *A theory of justice*, Oxford: Oxford University Press.

Reiner, R. (2006) 'Beyond risk: A lament for social democratic criminology', in T. Newburn and P. Rock (eds), *The politics of crime control*, Oxford: Oxford University Press.

Reiner, R. (2007) *Law and order: An honest citizen's guide to crime control*, Cambridge: Polity.

Rigakos, G. S. (2002) *The new parapolice: Risk markets and commodified social control*, Toronto: University of Toronto Press.

Rigakos, G. S. and Greener, D. R. (2000) 'Bubbles of governance: Private policing and the law in Canada', *Canadian Journal of Law and Society*, 15(1): 145–85.

Roach, K. (2004) 'The world wide expansion of anti-terrorism laws after 11 September 2001', *Studi Senesi*, 3: 487–527.

Roach, K. (2005) 'Miscarriages of justice in the war on terrorism', *Penn State Law Review*, 109(4): 967–1041.

Roberts, J. (2005) *Understanding public attitudes to criminal justice*, Milton Keynes: Open University Press.

Roche, D. (2003) *Accountability in restorative justice*, Oxford: Oxford University Press.

Rose, D. (2004) *Guantanamo: America's war on human rights*, London: Faber & Faber.

Rose, N. (1996) 'The death of the social? Reconfiguring the territory of government', *Economy and Society*, 25: 327–56.

Rose, N. (2000) 'Government and control', *British Journal of Criminology, Special Issue, Criminology and Social Theory*, 40: 321–39.

Rothman, D. (1971) *The discovery of the asylum: Social order and disorder in the new republic*, Boston: Little, Brown & Co.

Rothschild, E. (1995) 'What is security?', *Daedalus*, 123(3): 53–98.

Rudolph, C. (2003) 'Globalization and security: Migration and evolving conceptions of security in statecraft and scholarship', *Security Studies*, 13(1): 1–32.

Safferling, C. J. M. (2006) 'Law and terror', *Journal of International Criminal Justice*, 4(5): 1152–65.

Schneier, B. (2006) *Beyond fear: Thinking sensibly about security in an uncertain world*, New York: Springer.

Scott, A. (2000) 'Risk society or angst society? Two views of risk, consciousness and community', in B. Adam, U. Beck and J. van Loon (eds), *The risk society and beyond: Critical issues for social theory*, London: Sage, pp. 33–46.

Scott, C. (2004) 'Regulation in the age of governance: The rise of the post-regulatory state', in J. Jordana and D. Levi-Faur (eds), *The politics of regulation*, Cheltenham: Edward Elgar, 145–74.

Searle, G. R. (1971) *The quest for national efficiency: A study in British politics and political thought, 1899–1914*, Oxford: Basil Blackwell.

Semmel, B. (1960) *Imperialism and social reform: English social-imperial thought 1895–1914*, Cambridge, MA: Harvard University Press.

Shapland, J. and van Outrive, L. (eds) (1999) *Policing and security: Social control and the public–private divide*, Paris: Editions L'Harmattan.

Shearing, C. (2001a) 'A nodal conception of governance: Thoughts on a policing commission', *Policing and Society*, 11: 259–72.

Shearing, C. (2001b) 'Punishment and the changing face of governance', *Punishment and Society*, 3(2): 203–20.

Shearing, C. (2006) 'Reflections on the refusal to acknowledge private government', in J. Wood and B. Dupont (eds), *Democracy, society and the governance of security*, Cambridge: Cambridge University Press, pp. 11–32.

Shearing, C. and Johnston, L. (2005) 'Justice in the risk society', *Australian and New Zealand Journal of Criminology*, 38(1): 25–38.

Shearing, C. and Stenning, P. (1981) 'Modern private security: Its growth and implications', in M. Tonry and N. Morris (eds), *Crime and justice: An annual review of research*, Chicago: University of Chicago Press, vol. 3, pp. 193–245.

Shearing, C. and Stenning, P. (1983) 'Private security: Implications for social control', *Social Problems*, 30: 493–506.

Shearing, C. and Wood, J. (2003a) 'Governing security for common goods', *International Journal of Sociology of Law*, 31: 205–25.

Shearing, C. and Wood, J. (2003b) 'Nodal governance: Democracy, and the new "denizens" ', *Journal of Law and Society*, 30(3): 400–19.

Sheptycki, J. (2002) *In search of transnational policing: Towards a sociology of global policing*, Aldershot: Ashgate.

Shue, H. (1996) *Basic rights*, 2nd edn, Princeton: Princeton University Press.

Shue, H. and Rodin, D. (eds) (2007) *Preemption: Military action and moral justification*, Oxford: Oxford University Press.

Shute, S. (2004) 'New civil preventative orders: Sexual offences prevention orders, foreign travel orders and risk of sexual harm orders', *Criminal Law Review*, 417–40.

Sim, J. and Thomas, P. (1983) 'The Prevention of Terrorism Act: Normalising the politics of repression', *Journal of Law and Society*, 10(1): 71–84.

Simester, A. P. and von Hirsch, A. (2006) 'Regulating offensive conduct through two-step prohibitions', in A. P. Simester and A. von Hirsch (eds), *Incivilities: Regulating offensive behaviour*, Oxford: Hart Publishing, pp. 173–94.

Simon, J. (1997) 'Governing through crime', in L. M. Friedman and G. Fisher (eds), *The crime conundrum: Essays on criminal justice*, Boulder, CO: Westview Press.

Simon, J. (1998) 'Managing the monstrous: Sex offenders and the new penology', *Psychology, Public Policy and Law*, 3: 452–67.

Simon, J. (1999) 'From the big house to the warehouse: Rethinking state government and prisons', *Punishment and Society*, 3(2): 213–34.

Simon, J. (2000) 'The "society of captives" in the era of hyper-incarceration', *Theoretical Criminology*, 4(3): 285–308.

Simon, J. (2007) *Governing through crime: How the war on crime transformed American democracy and created a culture of fear*, New York: Oxford University Press.

Singer, P. W. (2003) *Corporate warriors: The rise of the privatized military industry*, New York: Cornell University Press.

Singh, A.-M. (2005) 'Private security and crime control', *Theoretical Criminology*, 9(2): 153–74.

Slobogin, C. (2003) 'A jurisprudence of dangerousness', *Northwestern University Law Review*, 98(1): 1–62.

Slobogin, C. (2005) 'The civilization of the criminal law', *Vanderbilt Law Review*, 58: 121–68.

Smith, A. (1978 [1762]) *Lectures on jurisprudence*, Oxford: Oxford University Press.

Sofaer, A. D. (2003) 'On the necessity of pre-emption', *European Journal of International Law*, 14(2): 209–26.

Sparks, R. (2000) 'Perspectives on risk and penal politics', in T. Hope and R. Sparks (eds), *Crime, risk and insecurity: Law and order in everyday life and political discourse*, London: Routledge, pp. 129–45.

Sparks, R. (2001) 'Degrees of estrangement: The cultural theory of risk and comparative penology', *Theoretical Criminology*, 5(2): 159–76.

Spitzer, S. (1987) 'Security and control in capitalist societies: The fetishism of security and the secret thereof', in J. Lowman, R. J. Menzies and T. S. Palys (eds), *Transcarceration: Essays in the sociology of social control*, Aldershot: Gower, pp. 43–58.

Spitzer, S. and Scull, A. (1977) 'Privatization and capitalist development: The case of the private police', *Social Problems*, 25: 18–29.

Stehr, N. and Ericson, R. (2000) 'The ungovernability of modern societies: States, democracies, markets, participation, and citizens', in R. Ericson and N. Stehr (eds), *Governing modern societies*, Toronto: University of Toronto Press, pp. 3–25.

Steiker, C. (1998) 'The limits of the preventive state', *Journal of Criminal Law and Criminology*, 88: 771–808.

Steiker, C. (2002) 'Civil and criminal divide', in J. Dressler (ed.), *Encyclopedia of crime and justice*, New York: Macmillan Reference, pp. 160–5.

Stenning, P. (2000) 'Powers and accountability of private police', *European Journal of Criminal Policy and Research*, 8(3): 325–52.

Stenson, K. (1996) 'Communal security as government: The British experience', in W. Hammersicht (ed.), *Jahrbuch für Rechts und Kriminalsoziologie*, Baden-Baden: Nomos, pp. 103–23.

Stenson, K. and Sullivan, R. R. (eds) (2001) *Crime, risk and justice: The politics of crime control in liberal democracies*, Cullompton: Willan Publishing.

Stern, J. and Wiener, J. B. (2006) 'Precaution against terrorism', *Journal of Risk Research*, 9(4): 393–447.

Stuntz, W. (2002) 'Local policing after the terror', *Yale Law Journal*, 111(8): 2137–94.

Sunstein, C. (2005) *Laws of fear: Beyond the precautionary principle*, Cambridge: Cambridge University Press.

Tadros, V. (2007a) *Criminal responsibility*, Oxford: Oxford University Press.

Tadros, V. (2007b) 'Justice and terrorism', *New Criminal Law Review*, 10(4): 658–89.

Taylor, I. (1998) 'Crime, market-liberalism and the European idea', in V. Ruggerio, N. South and I. Taylor (eds), *The new European criminology: Crime and social order in Europe*, London: Routledge, pp. 19–36.

Terriff, T., Croft, S., James, L. and Morgan, P. M. (2005) *Security studies today*, Cambridge: Polity.

Thomas, P. (2003) 'Emergency and anti-terrorist powers 9/11: USA and UK', *Fordham International Law Journal*, 26(4): 1193–233.

Tilly, C. (1985) 'War making and state making as organised crime', in P. Evans (ed.), *Bringing the state back in*, Cambridge: Cambridge University Press, pp. 169–91.

Titmuss, R. M. (1958) *Essays on the welfare state*, London: Allen & Unwin.

Tonry, M. (2007) *Crime, punishment and politics in comparative perspective: Crime and justice: A review of research*, Chicago: University of Chicago Press.

Tribe, L. and Gudridge, P. (2004) 'The anti-emergency constitution', *Yale Law Journal*, 113(8): 1801–70.

Tsoukala, A. (2004) 'Democracy against security: The debates about counter-terrorism in the European Parliament', *Alternatives*, 29: 417–39.

UN Commission on Human Security (2003) *Human security now*, New York: United Nations.

UNDP (United Nations Development Program) (1994) *New dimensions of human security*, New York: Oxford University Press.

Valverde, M. (2001) 'Governing security, governing through security', in R. Daniels, P. Macklem and K. Roach (eds), *The security of freedom: Essays on Canada's anti-terrorism bill*, Toronto: University of Toronto Press, pp. 83–92.

van Dijk, F. and de Waard, J. (2001a) 'The private security industry in the Netherlands', in F. Pakes and I. K. McKenzie (eds), *Law, power and justice in the Netherlands*, Westport: Greenwood Publishing.

van Dijk, F. and de Waard, J. (2001b) *Public and private crime control: National and international trends*, The Hague: Dutch Ministry of Justice.

Varese, F. (2001) *The Russian mafia: Private protection in a new market economy*. Oxford: Oxford University Press.

Vindevogel, F. (2005) 'Private security and urban crime mitigation: A bid for BIDs', *Criminal Justice*, 5(3): 233–55.

von Hirsch, A. (1993) *Censure and sanctions*, Oxford: Oxford University Press.

von Hirsch, A. and Ashworth, A. (2005) *Proportionate sentencing: Exploring the principles*, Oxford: Oxford University Press.

von Hirsch, A. and Shearing, C. (2000) 'Exclusion from public space', in

A. von Hirsch, D. Garland and A. Wakefield (eds), *Ethical and social perspectives on situational crime prevention*, Oxford: Hart Publishing, pp. 77–96.

von Hirsch, A. and Simester, A. P. (eds) (2006) *Incivilities: Regulating offensive behaviour*. Oxford: Hart Publishing.

Wadham, J. (2002) *Anti-terrorism legislation in the United Kingdom and the human rights concerns arising from it*, London: Liberty.

Waever, O. (1995) 'Securitization and desecuritization', in R. D. Lipschutz (ed.), *On security*, New York: Columbia University Press, pp. 46–86.

Wakefield, A. (2003) *Selling security: The private policing of public space*, Cullompton: Willan Publishing.

Waldron, J. (2003) 'Security and liberty: The image of balance', *Journal of Political Philosophy*, 11(2): 191–210.

Waldron, J. (2006) 'Safety and security', *Nebraska Law Review*, 85: 301–53.

Walker, C. (2004) 'Terrorism and criminal justice: Past, present and future', *Criminal Law Review*, 311–27.

Walker, N. (2003) 'The pattern of transnational policing', in T. Newburn (ed.), *Handbook of policing*, Cullompton: Willan Publishing, pp. 111–35.

Wall, D. (2007) *Cybercrime: The transformation of crime in the information age*, Cambridge: Polity.

Weber, L. (2007) 'Policing the virtual border: Punitive preemption in Australian offshore migration control', *Social Justice*, 34(2): 77–92.

Weiss, R. P. (1986) 'Private detective agencies and labour discipline in the United States, 1855–1946', *Historical Journal*, 29: 87–107.

Whitman, J. (2003) *Harsh justice: Criminal punishment and the widening divide between America and Europe*, Oxford: Oxford University Press.

Williams, J. W. (2005a) 'Governability matters: The private policing of economic crime and the challenge of democratic governance', *Policing and Society*, 15(2): 187–211.

Williams, J. W. (2005b) 'Reflections on the private versus public policing of economic crime', *British Journal of Criminology*, 45(3): 316–39.

Williams, P. D. (ed.) (2008) *Security studies: An introduction*, London: Routledge.

Wood, D. (2002) 'Retribution, crime reduction and the justification of punishment', *Oxford Journal of Legal Studies*, 22(2): 301–21.

Wood, J. (2006) 'Research and innovation in the field of security: A nodal governance view', in J. Wood and B. Dupont (eds), *Democracy, society and the governance of security*, Cambridge: Cambridge University Press, pp. 217–48.

Wood, J. and Shearing, C. (2007) *Imagining security*, Cullompton: Willan Publishing.

Woolford, A. (2006) 'Making genocide unthinkable: Three guidelines for a critical criminology of genocide', *Critical Criminology*, 14: 87–106.

Wyn-Jones, R. (1999) *Security, strategy, and critical theory*, London: Lynne Rienner.

Young, J. (1998) 'From inclusive to exclusive society: Nightmares in the European dream', in V. Ruggiero, N. South and I. Taylor (eds), *The new European criminology: Crime and social order in Europe*, London: Routledge.

Zedner, L. (2000) 'The pursuit of security', in T. Hope and R. Sparks (eds), *Crime, risk and insecurity: Law and order in everyday life and political discourse*, London: Routledge, pp. 200–14.

Zedner, L. (2003a) 'The concept of security: An agenda for comparative analysis', *Legal Studies*, 23(1): 153–76.

Zedner, L. (2003b) 'Too much security?', *International Journal of the Sociology of Law*, 31: 155–84.

Zedner, L. (2005) 'Securing liberty in the face of terror: Reflections from criminal justice', *Journal of Law and Society*, 32(4): 507–33.

Zedner, L. (2006a) 'Liquid security: Managing the market for crime control', *Criminology and Criminal Justice*, 6(2): 267–88.

Zedner, L. (2006b) 'Neither safe nor sound? The perils and possibilities of risk', *Canadian Journal of Criminology and Criminal Justice*, 48(3): 423–34.

Zedner, L. (2006c) 'Opportunity makes the thief-taker: The influence of economic analysis on crime control', in T. Newburn and P. Rock (eds), *The politics of crime control*, Oxford: Oxford University Press.

Zedner, L. (2006d) 'Policing before and after the police: The historical antecedents of contemporary crime control', *British Journal of Criminology*, 46(1): 78–96.

Zedner, L. (2007a) 'Pre-crime and post-criminology?', *Theoretical Criminology*, 11(2): 261–81.

Zedner, L. (2007b) 'Preventive justice or pre-punishment? The case of control orders', *Current Legal Problems*, 59: 174–203.

Zedner, L. (2007c) 'Seeking security by eroding rights: The side-stepping of due process', in B. Goold and L. Lazarus (eds), *Security and human rights*, Oxford: Hart Publishing.

Zedner, L. (2008a) 'The inescapable insecurity of security technologies?', in K. F. Aas, H. Oppen Gundhus and and H. Mork Lomell (eds), *Technologies of insecurity: The surveillance of everyday life*, London: Routledge.

Zedner, L. (2008b) 'Fixing the future? The pre-emptive turn in criminal justice', in S. Bronnit, B. McSherry and A. Norrie (eds), *Regulating deviance: The redirection of criminalisation and the futures of criminal law*, Oxford: Hart Publishing.

Zimring, F. E. and Hawkins, G. (1995) *Incapacitation: Penal confinement and the restraint of crime*, New York: Oxford University Press.

INDEX